Sweet
Christmas

Sweet Christmas

Homemade PEPPERMINTS, *Sugar* CAKE, *Chocolate-Almond* TOFFEE, *Eggnog* FUDGE, *and* Other SWEET TREATS *and* DECORATIONS

SHARON BOWERS

Photographs by DAVID BOWERS

STEWART, TABORI & CHANG, NEW YORK

For Hugh and Pearse, who make life sweet every day of the year

The goodies on page 1, clockwise from upper left: Peppermint Bark (page 21), Butter Mints (page 26), and Pamelas (page 35).

Published in 2012 by Stewart, Tabori & Chang
An imprint of ABRAMS

Library of Congress Cataloging-in-Publication Data:
Bowers, Sharon.
 Sweet Christmas / Sharon Bowers.
    p. cm.
 Includes index.
 ISBN 978-1-61769-000-6
1. Cookies. 2. Christmas cooking. 3. Christmas decorations. I.
Title.
 TX772.B68 2012
 641.5'686—dc23

Editor: Natalie Kaire with Elinor Hutton
Designer: Laura Klynstra
Production Manager: Kathy Lovisolo

The text of this book was composed in Filosofia and Gill Sans.

Printed and bound in China.
10 9 8 7 6 5 4 3 2 1

Stewart, Tabori & Chang books are available at special discounts when purchased in quantity for premiums and promotions as well as fundraising or educational use. Special editions can also be created to specification. For details, contact specialsales@abramsbooks.com or the address below.

THE ART OF BOOKS SINCE 1949
115 West 18th Street
New York, NY 10011
www.abramsbooks.com

Contents

'Tis the Season

After the publication of my first two books, my two sons and their friends, I regret to say, expected me to go nuts at Halloween and make all sorts of ghoulish goodies. They also required me to don my candy-foreman's cap and oversee candy construction at birthday parties and special events. But that's the problem with being known as a mom who has truck with sweet stuff. The ante keeps getting upped, and after a while, everyone under the age of ten wonders why you're not busting a move at Christmastime, too.

Happily, Christmas is the time of year when I *most* want to get into the kitchen and open the sugar bin. Homemade candy seems like too much trouble for about eleven months of the year, but in December, every moment I spend watching a candy thermometer seems worth it when people's eyes light up at the sight of that tin of homemade butter mints or that paper twist filled with sugared pecans. Extra effort when it comes to cupcake toppers or cookie décor is in order in December, as well; it's nice to have an opportunity to show off a little if you've actually bothered to make cream puffs and glue them together with frosting and chocolate sauce so they look like a Christmas tree.

Like a lot of people, however, I occupy that space somewhere between extremely busy and very lazy; it's amazing how often the two go together. I can't be the only mom who finds that after a long day of working, managing my family's domestic bliss, and the constant picking up and dropping off of children, I'd rather collapse on the sofa than start a new project.

Because of that feeling, I need my Christmas projects to offer some real bang for my buck, or I'm not going to bother. For example, should you take the time to caramelize onions and make homemade onion dip for a Christmas Eve gathering instead of zipping open a packet of onion soup mix? *Ohhh, yes, a thousand times yes.* On the other hand, other projects are kind of nifty and cool for *not* a lot of extra effort. Unwrap white cupcakes, frost them all over with white icing, and roll them in flaked coconut and luster sugar for fabulous-looking snowballs . . . kids will look at you like you just invented sliced white bread.

I'm also a big believer in using what's simplest and close at hand, so you don't have to buy a pastry bag when a zip-top storage bag with a hole cut in one corner will do, and you don't need a lot of special cookie cutters if you've got a paring knife and a steady hand. And while I give recipes for homemade cupcakes and frosting on different projects, know that a cake mix can sometimes be the busy baker's best friend. Choose your battles, I say.

That said, choosing to make homemade goodies *is* one of the personal battles I've fought and won during the holidays. As the years go by, I've found that creating and giving homemade gifts is much less expensive than singlehandedly making my local mall prosperous each December—and it's also much more satisfying—to me, to my family, and to the recipients of our efforts. My husband and I have found that when we're not galloping from store to store, whiny children in tow, seeking the perfect (usually elusive) present, then the whole holiday season passes more calmly, more enjoyably. We actually have, and take, the time on a dark Friday winter evening to go into the kitchen and make pulled ribbon candy, which leaves my kids delirious with joy.

It's a matter of not thinking of our kitchen efforts as work but as part of the seasonal pleasure. So rather than watch TV after school (I mean, um, sit quietly and do homework),

my boys are very happy to flop down and tie the ends of wrapped candy into endless garlands to loop over doorframes or around the Christmas tree and to mold little "Santa mice" out of sticky chocolate dough.

Get into the kitchen and create some new taste memories and traditions. Children will enjoy the holiday season that much more, and your whole family will have fun in the process.

Notes on Ingredients

Butter

Throughout this book, the recipes call for "butter," and by that I mean salted butter. Salted butter is what I buy to eat, it's in my refrigerator when I go to bake, and it usually contains enough salt that you don't need to add any more (or only a very little bit) to the recipe. If you're starting with unsalted butter, you may need a pinch of additional salt in a recipe to make it taste balanced. Even sugary dishes need a little salt to temper their sweetness and keep them from tasting flat.

Chocolate

My kitchen cabinets usually contain chocolate chips, so for everyday recipes, I rarely look much farther. To melt them successfully, put them in a microwave-safe bowl and microwave them on high for 1 minute, then stir vigorously with a fork. If the mixture isn't smooth by then, let it sit for a moment or two—you may find that the residual heat will melt the remaining lumps, but if it requires more time, heat the chocolate only in 10-second blasts, stirring and letting it rest between each zap. This is especially important with white chocolate chips, which are inclined to seize up into a stiff, ruined mass at the slightest provocation.

For several recipes here, I've specified when better chocolate might be worth the effort. But I'm not suggesting you need to special-order Callebaut or Valrhona or look for rare brands at gourmet stores. Nearly all supermarkets now have Ghirardelli's in their baking sections, and the 60% and 70% cacao versions will, for

cooking, always give you an excellent result. Scharffen Berger is also widely available, and each of these is a *major* step up from "baking chocolate" (or chocolate chips!).

When unsweetened cocoa powder is called for, any brand of regular or Dutch process powder is usually fine. High-end name-brand cocoa powders make a bigger difference when you're tasting them in frosting, cocoa, or pudding, but for baking, a lot of those subtleties can be lost.

Eggs

When a recipe calls for eggs, large eggs are ideal, but these recipes aren't so finely calibrated that using small, medium, or jumbo eggs will ruin it.

Extracts and Oils

I like to use only pure extracts, such as real vanilla and real almond flavoring, to avoid the chemical aftertaste fake extracts can have. When working with peppermint specifically, there's quite a difference between using food-grade peppermint essential oil and peppermint extract, and for some recipes, such as mints, there will be different measurements depending on whether you're using extract or oil.

Flour

For most of my home baking, I use unbleached all-purpose flour. I love soft white Southern flour, such as White Lily, for making cakes and sweets, since it produces such a tender product. I'm also a huge fan of whole wheat pastry flour, which is milled extra-fine and can be used in place of white flour in cakes, cookies, and quick breads. When making breads and hearty cookies such as oatmeal, I sometimes use up to 50 percent stoneground whole wheat flour, but for the indulgent holiday recipes in this book, white flour is usually the best option.

Measurements

I dislike over-fussy measurements in recipes. I think food is pretty forgiving and adjustable to personal taste, so I'll never call for 1⅛ teaspoon, for example, when 1 teaspoon will do just fine. If you want a little extra cinnamon or a little less sugar, these recipes are all amenable to that. However, if a recipe recommends you boil something to a certain temperature, it's probably a good idea to do it (see Thermometer, page 11). And here's a recommendation for anyone who wonders why cookies always burn, or seem to be raw, at the recommended time in the recipe: Use your nose. Depending on your oven (mine is a little "fast," as they used to say, or over-hot), your baking time could be five or ten minutes off the recipe's stated time. So when you start to smell "finished cookie," open the oven and check it out, and stand by until they're ready—it will only be another minute or two.

Milk

My household drinks 1% milk, which is a compromise between my desire for skim and a spouse who grew up drinking only whole milk (of such most marriages are made, no?). And so that's what I tend to cook with, and whatever milk *you* have in the refrigerator is probably fine. If using whole milk will make an appreciable difference (as in the Drinking Custard, page 111), I recommend it. But you're free to ignore me and use what you have with impunity.

Molasses

Can you tell me the difference between sulfured and unsulfured molasses? Yes? Well, then, you probably also have a very definite opinion on which one is best for any given recipe and require no further commentary from me. All the rest of us may continue to use whatever is in the kitchen cabinet, since we know our gingerbread men come out fine every time.

Sugar

In these recipes, "sugar" means granulated white sugar. Also, I know it's laissez-faire at best, heresy to professional bakers at worst, but I tend to use light brown and dark brown sugar interchangeably in my own kitchen. Here I've bowed to convention and called for whichever of the two will best suit the recipe, but if all you've got is dark brown when the recipe says light, go ahead and use it. I'll never tell.

Notes on Equipment

Parchment Paper

As casual as I am about using chocolate chips where another cook would use couverture, I'm adamant about the importance of parchment paper in baking. Wax paper is *not* the same thing, nor is foil. When either of those less-expensive options will work, I specify their use in the recipe. But if the recipe calls for parchment or a silicone liner, don't substitute something else or you'll likely end up with a sticky mess. The highest grades of parchment paper, the sheets that professionals use, are coated with a layer of silicone, and they can be wiped off and reused over and over. But even the thinnest parchment paper available by the roll in the supermarket has a thin layer of a nonstick coating that makes it much more effective than a greased baking sheet. If you're not in the habit, buy a roll—you'll never look back.

Silicone Mats

Although I don't usually call for them in a recipe, you can use silicone mats anywhere parchment is specified. They're thick nonstick mats that you can lay on a baking sheet and use—well, forever, it seems. Silpat is the best-known brand. I am not even close to wearing out my Silpat after some ten years of baking on it. However, even more nonstick is my inexpensive no-name silicone mat, much thinner than my plushy Silpat, that I can wipe off and refold. As long as it's silicone, the name brand shouldn't matter.

Spatulas

Heatproof silicone spatulas and scrapers are favorite tools of mine. They tend to be sturdier and longer-lasting than old-fashioned rubber scrapers, and you can use them to stir a pot of boiling sugar without risk of them melting. The best ones are flexible but still sturdy, so you can easily scrape out the last cake batter or cookie dough from a bowl.

Thermometer

Don't boil sugar or oil without a candy/deep-frying thermometer. It's an inexpensive piece of equipment, and it's completely indispensable. Get the kind with a clip that lets you affix it to the side of the pan so you can keep a constant eye on the temperature.

Notes on Storage

Airtight Containers

Homemade candy tends to be particularly susceptible to humidity, so many of these recipes call for storing the treats in an airtight container. Ideally, that's a plastic tub or a metal tin with a tight-fitting lid. But don't despair if you don't have either. You can also store them very successfully in a gallon-size zip-top storage bag.

Freezing

Many of these treats can be made in advance and frozen. As a general rule, the best candidates for freezing are items like cookies and bars, things with flour as a key ingredient. Items without flour, such as chocolate-dipped candied orange peels, will freeze less successfully because the moisture that will collect on them as they thaw can ruin the integrity of the sweet. Chocolate, such as chocolate truffles, can be frozen, but be aware that chocolate stored at low temperatures is prone to "bloom"—when the cocoa solids rise to the surface in white or light patches. Bloom usually fades when the chocolate returns to room temperature. Though it's not pretty, it's completely harmless.

Packing

If you're mailing any of these goodies, popcorn (yes, *real* popcorn) is an excellent packing material that will absorb moisture, provide cushioning against bumps and shocks, and also avoid imparting odd flavors the way plastic packing materials might. Some people argue that filling a mailer with popcorn puts it at risk for bugs, but if you're shipping a boxful of sugary treats anyway, that point seems kind of moot. Just tell the recipient not to eat the popcorn.

Refrigeration

Don't assume that putting something in the refrigerator will keep it dry. Although the fridge can help chill and firm up some candies, such as chocolate bark or just-boiled toffee, in the short term, it's actually quite humid in there, and for long-term storage, it can have the adverse effect of making your stored sweets limp and moist.

Pamelas page 35

Sugared Pecans page 32

CHAPTER ONE

Holiday Classics

❋

Christmas Candy
to Make at Home

Candy-making at home sounds intimidating, but this is not the kind that requires tempered chocolate and molds painted with glycerin. Instead, it's the sort of old-fashioned candy that our grandmothers used to make: divinity, boiled sweets, toffee. Some will require an inexpensive candy thermometer—pulled-ribbon candy, for example, which is ambitious enough to be an evening's entertainment for the whole family—whereas for butter mints, you don't even need to apply heat to get a sweet, creamy treat.

That's not to say that I don't like things dipped in chocolate as well, of course, but above all I do like straightforward, if not downright simple, recipes. Tempering chocolate—a complicated system of heating and cooling it to specific temperatures to achieve a smooth texture and glossy finish—was for the days before I had children, and I can honestly say I have not attempted to do it since my first child was born. What I do now is reach for the bag of chocolate chips that's generally sitting in my cupboards somewhere, and melt that whenever I want to coat something in chocolate.

The lazy (busy) woman's method of "tempering" is to add a tablespoon of vegetable oil or, even better, solid vegetable shortening, to the chocolate as it melts in the microwave or double-boiler; this will make the finished product glossy and shiny. You can do the same trick successfully even with higher-quality chocolate, such as the Ghirardelli 60% or 70% cacao bars that are available in any supermarket's baking section.

Maybe my standards haven't slipped so far after all! All I know is, no one has ever turned down any of the candy treats in this chapter.

Christmas Divinity

Makes about 1 pound candy

Southerners love divinity, which is kind of funny when you consider that people who live in one of the hottest, most humid parts of the United States like a candy that simply cannot be made in humid weather: The divinity will simply languish on the baking sheet, soggy and refusing to firm up. That's probably why it always appears on Christmas buffets and in gift boxes. The cold, crisp December air helps make each sugary puff as fluffy and light as possible. I like chopped pecans throughout the mixture, but you can skip the chopping and press an entire pecan half on top of each puff. Walnuts are good here, too.

2½ cups sugar

½ cup light corn syrup

½ cup warm water

2 egg whites

1½ teaspoons vanilla extract

1 cup chopped pecans

1. Line a baking sheet with parchment paper. Combine the sugar, corn syrup, and water in a large, heavy saucepan over medium heat. Cook, stirring constantly, until the sugar dissolves. Continue cooking without stirring until the mixture reaches 250°F.

2. While the sugar is cooking, beat the egg whites in a stand mixer until stiff peaks form. (You can use a hand mixer, but a stand mixer makes adding the sugar syrup easier.) With the mixer running, very, very slowly drizzle in half the sugar syrup directly from the saucepan.

3. Return the saucepan to the heat and continue cooking the remaining syrup for a few more minutes until the mixture reaches 270°F.

4. With the mixer running, drizzle the remaining syrup into the egg whites. Continue to beat at a medium speed until the divinity is glossy and thick. Depending on the weather, this can take anywhere from 5 to 15 minutes.

5. Once the divinity thickens and looks shiny (and will hold its shape), beat in the vanilla and nuts.

6. Working quickly, use a pair of teaspoons to drop dollops of divinity onto the parchment paper, using one spoon to push the candy off the other. If you're a pro, you may be able to make a swirl on top of each candy with the back of the spoon. Let sit until firm. Store the divinity in an airtight container for up to 1 week.

Baked Pralines

fragile, crisp, and lovely to behold   *Makes about 2 dozen pralines*

"Real" pralines are an exquisite concoction of boiled sugar and butter with nuts dropped onto paper in dabs. "Baked" pralines are a completely different item—more like an extremely delicate cookie—but they still fall under the heading "confection" because of their incredibly thin, crackling shells. They're almost like a French macaron *in the way they puff. Plan to serve them within a day or two of making them because humidity is their enemy.*

  8 ounces (about 2 cups) pecan halves
  2 egg whites
  2 cups light brown sugar
  2 tablespoons all-purpose flour
  ¼ teaspoon salt
  1½ teaspoons vanilla extract

1. Preheat the oven to 275°F and line two baking sheets with parchment paper.

2. Put the pecan halves in the food processor and pulse two to three times to chop them very coarsely. (You can also do this by hand.) Don't process them to a paste. Set aside.

3. In a medium bowl, beat the egg whites with a hand mixer, until they are stiff but not dry. Add all the remaining ingredients to the egg whites, folding them in with a wide spatula. Fold in the chopped nuts.

4. Drop heaping teaspoons of the mixture by 2 inches apart on the prepared baking sheets (you should be able to get all the cookies onto the prepared sheets). Bake the pralines for 25 to 30 minutes, until they're crisp and puffed. Cool the pralines completely before carefully removing them from the parchment. Store them in an airtight container for a day or two (they'll still taste good a few days later, but they won't have that delicate crust).

Creamy Eggnog Fudge

Makes about 2 pounds fudge

Once I discovered the ease of making fudge with marshmallow cream, I never looked back. I'd spent too many years madly beating the boiled-sugar-and-cocoa kind, only to have it refuse to set up. So marshmallow cream (I do prefer the Fluff brand, if only from force of habit) has become my magic ingredient. The eggnog in this recipe is more of a nod to the flavor than a necessity, since the "eggnog" taste really comes from the nutmeg, vanilla, and rum extract. So if you don't have any eggnog left in your fridge, you can make this with evaporated milk or cream.

2 cups sugar

2 cups (7 ounces) marshmallow cream

½ cup (1 stick) butter

½ cup store-bought eggnog (preferably the full-fat kind)

2 cups (12 ounces) white chocolate chips

1 teaspoon vanilla extract

1 teaspoon rum extract (or 2 tablespoons dark rum)

½ teaspoon freshly grated nutmeg, plus a bit more for the topping

1. Line a 9-inch square pan with foil, letting a few inches hang over the sides. Lightly grease the foil and the sides of the pan with butter.

2. In a large, heavy saucepan over medium heat, mix the sugar, marshmallow cream, butter, and eggnog. Bring to a boil, stirring constantly. Boil for 5 minutes, until the mixture registers 234°F on a candy thermometer.

3. Remove the pan from the heat and add the white chocolate chips. Stir until they are melted and fully incorporated, then add the vanilla, rum extract, and nutmeg.

4. Turn the fudge into the pan and immediately top it with a generous grating of additional nutmeg, patting it gently with the back of a spoon (or the tips of your fingers) to lightly press the nutmeg into the surface. Cover, and chill until firm. Run a knife around the edge of the pan to loosen the fudge, and cut it into 1-inch squares. Store in an airtight container in the refrigerator for up to 2 weeks.

Peppermint Fudge

Makes about 2 pounds fudge

This is as easy as the eggnog fudge, but this time it's dark chocolate with a minty kick. The crushed candy canes (or those round pinwheel peppermint candies) add crunch and texture. Break the candy up in the food processor, being careful not to overprocess it to a powder, or seal the candy in a heavy, gallon-size zip-top storage bag and let the kids crush it with the bottom of a heavy mug.

2 cups sugar

2 cups (7 ounces) marshmallow cream

¾ cup (5 ounces) evaporated milk

5 tablespoons butter

¼ teaspoon salt

2 cups (12 ounces) semisweet chocolate chips

1 cup crushed candy canes or peppermint candies

½ teaspoon peppermint extract

1. Line a 9-inch square pan with foil, letting a few inches hang over the sides. Lightly grease the foil and the sides of the pan with butter.

2. In a large, heavy saucepan over medium heat, combine the sugar, marshmallow cream, evaporated milk, butter, and salt. Bring the mixture to a boil, stirring to dissolve the sugar, and cook until the temperature reaches 234°F on a candy thermometer, about 5 minutes.

3. Pour in the chocolate chips and half of the crushed candy, stirring until the chocolate is melted. Add the peppermint extract, stir, and turn the fudge into the prepared pan. Sprinkle the remaining crushed candy over the surface, pressing it down lightly so it sticks.

4. Chill the fudge until set, then cut it into 1-inch squares. Store it in an airtight container in the refrigerator for up to 1 week. (Note that if your container isn't airtight, the humidity in the fridge may cause the crushed candy on top to soften.)

Peppermint Bark

If you've ever purchased chocolate bark, you'll probably feel a little foolish when you make it at home for the first time: it's that easy, the candymaker's equivalent of boiling water. Using chocolate chips is fine, but you can also use your favorite gourmet chocolate instead. (You can also buy very cheap chunks of chocolate labeled "bark." This type of chocolate usually has no cocoa solids—but it works well!) If you are using chips, stirring a tiny bit of vegetable oil into the melted chocolate makes for a smoother, glossier finish.

Bark is endlessly forgiving and you can vary it as you like: Use only one type of chocolate and make a single layer, or skip the peppermint extract and candy and stir in 1 cup of dried fruit and 1 cup of chopped nuts (such as dried cranberries and chopped pistachios—sprinkle some nuts and fruit on top as well), or use white chocolate chips and butterscotch chips and sprinkle crushed butterscotch candies on the top.

2 cups (12 ounces) semisweet chocolate chips

4 teaspoons vegetable oil

2 teaspoons peppermint extract

2 cups (12 ounces) white chocolate chips

1½ cups crushed peppermint candies or candy canes

1. Line a rimmed baking sheet with parchment paper or lightly buttered foil.

2. Put the semisweet chips in a microwavable bowl and nuke them for 2 minutes on high. The chips may still appear whole at this point, but they will quickly dissolve. Stir vigorously, adding in 2 teaspoons of the oil and 1 teaspoon of the peppermint extract, and continuing to beat the chips until they're smooth. You may not need any more melting time, but if you do, put the bowl back in the microwave for 10-second bursts, stirring between each, to avoid scorching the chocolate.

3. Pour the melted chocolate onto the prepared pan, spreading it with a rubber spatula. Firm it up in the refrigerator for 10 minutes.

4. Following the directions in Step 2, melt the white chips. Add the remaining oil and peppermint extract, then pour over the chocolate bark. Quickly sprinkle the top with the crushed peppermint candies so they stick to the melted chocolate. Firm up in the refrigerator for 10 minutes, then break the bark into chunks. Store the bark in an airtight container at room temperature for up to 1 week.

White Chocolate, Cherry, and Pistachio Drops

Makes about 2½ dozen candies

These are like bark but fancier, since you spoon them into individual drops, which makes for good candy to bag up as a gift or to present in little paper cups on a dessert table. They have that slightly lumpy homemade finish that says, "I made it myself!" (In a good way, of course.) Macadamias also taste good here, but then you won't get that subtle holiday red-and-green combo of cherries and pistachios. If you have one of those pricey little bottles of pure orange oil, this is the place to use it. Otherwise, orange zest adds a lovely flavor.

2 cups (12 ounces) white chocolate chips
¼ teaspoon pure orange oil or the grated zest of 1 orange
1 cup dried cherries (or dried cranberries), plus more for garnish, if desired
½ cup chopped pistachios, plus more for garnish, if desired

1. Line a rimmed baking sheet with parchment paper or lightly buttered foil.

2. Put the white chocolate chips in a microwavable bowl and nuke them for 1 minute on high. The chips may still appear whole at this point, but they will quickly dissolve. Stir vigorously, adding in the oil and continuing to beat the chips until they're smooth. You may not need any more melting time, but if you do, microwave the chocolate in 10-second bursts, stirring between each, to avoid scorching it.

3. Blend in the orange oil or zest, then add the cherries and pistachios. Working quickly, use a pair of teaspoons to drop spoonfuls onto the prepared pan. (If you like, press additional cherries, pistachios, orange zest, or a combination, on top of each drop.) Let the drops sit until firm, or firm them up in the refrigerator. Store them in an airtight container for up to 1 week.

Homemade Ribbon Candy

One Christmas during my childhood, someone gave my family a huge tin of ribbon candy, each piece set into elaborate squiggles just like curled ribbon. There were solid colors and stripes, too, and to be honest, it didn't even taste that great, but my siblings and I were enchanted with it, and we ate every last shard. (To a kid, sugar is sugar, after all.) Only in recent years have I had the nerve to try making my own ribbon candy, however, since all the hot sugar seemed intimidating. Imagine my surprise when I discovered that it's not very hard and it's wildly fun. This is a great family project for a Friday evening.

Make sure everyone has a pair of disposable plastic gloves so no little fingers get burned. You'll also definitely need a candy thermometer and a metal dough scraper or large metal spatula. You also need a lot of pans to hold all that hot sugar as you work. If you don't have that many baking sheets, press other large pans, such as a roasting pan or a 9-by-13-inch baking dish, into service.

Vegetable oil

3 cups sugar

1 cup light corn syrup

1 teaspoon pure peppermint oil (or 2 teaspoons peppermint extract)

Red and green food coloring (liquid or paste)

1. Preheat the oven to 185°F. Dip a wadded-up paper towel in vegetable oil and grease four baking sheets.

2. In a large, heavy saucepan over medium heat, combine the sugar, corn syrup, and ¼ cup water. Bring the mixture to a boil, stirring continuously until the sugar has dissolved. Then allow it to boil, without stirring, until it reaches 300°F (hard-crack stage) on a candy thermometer.

3. Quickly stir in the peppermint oil and pour one-third of the mixture onto the first prepared sheet. Pour another third of the mixture into a second sheet and the rest into a third sheet. Drop 4 drops of red food coloring atop the candy on one sheet, and 4 drops of green coloring on another. Set the uncolored sheet and the green sheet into the warm oven.

4. Wet a dish towel and wring it out. Fold it in half and spread it on a clean work surface. Place the red baking sheet on top of the dish towel to prevent it from sliding around on the counter. Let the candy sit for a few minutes until it cools enough to have a sort of crust or skin on top. Use a little vegetable oil to grease both sides of a metal dough scraper or a large metal spatula, and use this to push and pull the candy, spreading it around the baking sheet to incorporate the red food coloring.

5. After a few minutes of this mixing, the candy should have cooled *just* enough for you to handle it. Put on plastic gloves and lightly grease your gloved hands with vegetable oil. Pick up the whole

hunk of hot sugar (or use a sharp knife to cut it into 2 or 3 pieces and hand a chunk to each child). Pull it between your hands (or, more fun, pull it between 2 people), stretching it out and folding it back on itself, twisting the candy into a rope that you then pull again. Pull and twist for 3 to 4 minutes, until the candy is no longer transparent and the color permeates it; it will have cooled and started to firm up. If you mixed pieces separately, recombine them into a thick rope and place it back on the baking sheet. Put it into the warm oven and repeat the process with the remaining 2 baking sheets. (The candy without any coloring will turn white and opaque as you pull it.)

6. Use the vegetable oil to lightly grease the blades of a pair of clean kitchen shears. Cut a short length of candy off of each rope and return all the baking sheets to the oven so the ropes remain pliable. Pull each cut piece into a 6-inch strip. Lay the 3 strips side by side and begin pulling them together. Gently twist and mold to make a tricolor candy ribbon. When you get the look you like, pull it into as thin a ribbon as possible and cut 6-inch lengths with the greased scissors. Curl them into a ribbon shape and lay them gently on the fourth prepared baking sheet to firm up at room temperature.

7. Repeat with all the remaining candy, making any color combinations you like. Any time the candy gets too firm to mold, set it back in the warm oven for a few minutes. When you're finished, let all the finished ribbons cool to room temperature to firm up, then store them in zip-top storage bags, pushing out as much air as possible before sealing them so the candy doesn't get sticky from any humidity in the air. As long they stay dry, they'll keep indefinitely.

Butter Mints

When I was a child, people made butter mints for two occasions: weddings and Christmas. Wedding mints came in various pastel tints: pink, yellow, blue. But Christmas ones were only green, a creamy hue that hinted at the delicate flavor of the handmade treat. Back then, they were the province of little old ladies and maiden aunts, but they were always the first thing to disappear off a buffet table—one of those goodies whose simple ingredients belied their addictive taste. These get better after sitting in their tins for a few days, as the mint flavor melds with the butter and blooms, and the confectioners' sugar loses its raw taste.

I pound (about 4 cups) confectioners' sugar, plus more for tossing
$\frac{1}{2}$ cup (1 stick) butter, softened
I teaspoon pure peppermint oil (or 2 teaspoons peppermint extract)
Green food coloring

1. Line a couple of baking sheets with wax paper. Put the sugar and butter in a large bowl and rub them together with your fingers. (You can use a fork, but clean hands work best, also making this an ideal job for any young person who may be hanging about your kitchen.)

2. Stir the peppermint oil and 2 drops of green food coloring into 1 tablespoon of water (to help distribute the flavor and color) and sprinkle this over the surface of the butter and sugar. Stir to combine, then pour the contents of the bowl onto a clean work surface and knead with your hands until a firm dough is formed. If you absolutely must, you can add up to 1 tablespoon of water more, but do this 1 teaspoon at a time. (If you get this dough too wet, there's no going back. Better to knead for a moment or two and see if it comes together before resorting to extra water.) Continue to knead for several minutes until the dough is elastic and shiny.

3. Divide the dough into quarters and roll each into a ball. Set 3 dough pieces aside, covered with a sheet of plastic wrap or a damp, well-wrung dish towel. Roll each ball out into a long rope about $\frac{1}{2}$ inch in diameter. Use a sharp kitchen knife to cut it into $\frac{1}{2}$-inch lengths, so each mint is a little squarish pillow, pinched at each end, and lay the cut mints on the prepared baking sheets. Continue until you've cut all the remaining dough.

4. Let the mints rest, uncovered, at room temperature for several hours, until they are firm and dry to the touch, shaking the sheets now and then to roll them around so they dry on all sides. Store them in airtight tins (or plastic zip-top storage bags with the air pressed out, if you don't have tins) for up to 2 weeks at room temperature, or up to 3 months in the freezer. If the mints seem moist, toss them with a few tablespoons of confectioners' sugar before serving.

Crispy Christmas Toffee

buttery, crisp, melting, almond-topped

Makes about 1 pound toffee

So many toffee recipes are disappointing—too chewy or not very crisp. What I want is that tender caramel flavor that breaks easily under your teeth, like . . . well, store-bought toffee. What you need is a tiny hint of baking soda, so the toffee puffs up but doesn't become spongy. This is that recipe, in all its buttery, sugary glory, with nuts and a sprinkle of flaky salt, for that classy salted-caramel taste. Kosher salt is fine, but if you're trying to impress someone, use fleur de sel or Maldon sea salt, and be sure to mention it!

½ cup (1 stick) butter

1½ cups sugar

1 tablespoon light corn syrup

1 teaspoon vanilla extract

⅛ teaspoon baking soda

½ cup finely chopped almonds

½ teaspoon kosher salt (or any flaky sea salt, but *not* iodized table salt)

1. Line a rimmed baking sheet with foil and lightly butter it (or use parchment, which won't require buttering). In a large, heavy saucepan over medium heat, combine the butter, sugar, 3 tablespoons of water, and the corn syrup, stirring until the sugar dissolves. Continue to cook without stirring until the mixture reaches 300°F (hard-crack stage) on a candy thermometer.

2. Quickly stir in the vanilla and baking soda (the mixture will foam) and pour the toffee onto the prepared baking sheet, spreading it thin with a silicone spatula.

3. Sprinkle the finely chopped nuts evenly over the top of the hot toffee, and then sprinkle the salt over, holding your hand 8 to 10 inches above the toffee as you do this to help the salt cover the surface evenly and to avoid salty clumps.

4. Let the toffee firm up at room temperature (you can speed this up by placing it in the refrigerator, but too much humidity isn't good for toffee, so remove it as soon as the toffee is hard, after 20 minutes or so). Break it into pieces and store it in an airtight container for up to 2 weeks.

Saltine Chocolate-Almond Toffee

down and dirty, quick and delicious   *Makes about 2 pounds toffee*

This is one of those recipes that spreads like wildfire around the Internet, mainly because it's one of those miraculous foods that you can't believe is so good. If you don't have time to wait for traditional toffee to boil to the hard-crack stage and then firm up, this is your recipe. Kids love to lay the crackers out on the baking sheet, like a giant puzzle, while you boil the sugar and butter. The chocolate on top makes it addictively tasty, and you can use any nut here; chopped peanuts are particularly good.

> 40 salted soda crackers (about 1½ sleeves)
> 1 cup (2 sticks) butter
> 1 cup dark brown sugar
> 2 cups (12 ounces) semisweet chocolate chips
> 1 cup thinly sliced almonds (or any nut you like)

1. Preheat the oven to 400°F and line a rimmed baking sheet with parchment paper or buttered foil.

2. Place the crackers on the baking sheet in a single layer. In a small saucepan, bring the butter and brown sugar to a boil. When it begins to boil, let it bubble furiously for 3 minutes. Pour the toffee over the crackers and bake them for 5 minutes.

3. Remove the toffee from the oven and sprinkle the chocolate chips over the top. Let it sit for a minute or two, then use a silicone spatula to spread the melting chocolate evenly over the surface.

4. Sprinkle the chocolate layer evenly with the chopped nuts and then let it cool. When it's completely cool and firm, break it into pieces. Store the toffee in an airtight container at room temperature for up to 1 week.

Chocolate-Covered Cherries

Makes about 3 dozen candies

Society divides pretty evenly into people who like chocolate-covered cherries and those who don't, into those who buy and eat them by the boxful and those who accidentally bite into one in a sampler and hastily tuck it back, hoping nobody will notice. I'm the latter, married to the former, inexplicably enough, and if I have to eat one, the homemade version is vastly superior to the kind my husband occasionally buys at the drugstore. Don't worry about putting a little extra fat or shortening in the chocolate—it's just a trick to make the finished coating smoother and shinier without complicated "tempering." Some people use food-grade paraffin instead. You can skip it, if you like, but your candy may not be as pretty. The stem on the cherry makes the perfect dipping handle, but if yours don't have stems, use a toothpick to dip each one, then dab a little chocolate over the hole where you remove the toothpick to make an airtight chocolate shell. Make the cherries about 1 week before you want to serve them to let the fondant centers liquefy in their chocolate shells.

1 jar (20 ounces) maraschino cherries with stems, in heavy syrup

2 cups confectioners' sugar, plus a little more as needed

3 tablespoons butter, softened

2 tablespoons corn syrup

1/4 teaspoon pure almond extract (optional)

3 cups (18 ounces) semisweet chocolate chips (or about 1 pound "coating" chocolate, such as dark chocolate bark)

1 tablespoon solid vegetable shortening or vegetable oil

1. Reserve 1 tablespoon of the cherry juice, then drain the cherries and gently pat them dry with paper towels, being careful to leave the stems attached. Let them sit on paper towels while you prepare the fondant. Line two baking sheets with wax or parchment paper.

2. In a medium bowl, combine the confectioners' sugar, butter, corn syrup, reserved cherry liquid, and the almond extract, if using. Stir to blend. Turn the mixture out onto a clean work surface and knead until it is smooth and pliable, adding 1 or 2 more tablespoons confectioners' sugar if needed to make a firm fondant. (If your kitchen is very warm, you may need to chill it for 30 minutes in the refrigerator to stiffen it up.)

3. Wrap about 1½ teaspoons of fondant all the way around each cherry. Line up the covered cherries on the prepared baking sheets and place them in the freezer for about 30 minutes to firm up.

4. While the cherries are chilling, melt the chocolate and the shortening or oil in a double boiler, stirring frequently. Turn off the heat, but keep the chocolate over the warm water.

5. Holding each cherry by the stem, dip it in the chocolate, turning it to coat all sides. Place the cherry back on the baking sheet; repeat the process until all are dipped (you may need to tip the chocolate container a bit toward the end so each cherry gets fully covered). Store them in a single layer in airtight containers at room temperature for up to 1 month.

Sugared Pecans

Pecans were the nut of choice when I grew up, and we used to get them by the brown-paper sackful from my great-uncle's farm in Tennessee, where he had acres of pecan groves. So I am always a little surprised when I have to dip into the kids' college fund to buy several pounds of them at Christmastime, but they're worth it. They're one of the sweetest nuts, not terribly crunchy but with a sturdy, almost meaty texture, and they're a classic Christmas treat when toasted with a little sweet-spicy sugar coating. The ideal way to portion them out is in a cone of thick brown paper or parchment paper, perhaps with an outer layer of bright wrapping paper (you need that grease-proof inner lining). Roll a 12-inch square of paper into a cone, tape the side to hold its shape, then scoop in a generous half cup of the cooled pecans and twist the top shut.

- 1 egg white
- 1 teaspoon vanilla extract
- 4 cups (about 1 pound) pecan halves
- 1 cup sugar
- 1 teaspoon kosher salt (or ½ teaspoon table salt)
- ½ teaspoon ground cinnamon
- ½ teaspoon freshly grated nutmeg

1. Preheat the oven to 300°F and lightly butter a rimmed baking sheet.

2. In a large bowl, vigorously whisk the egg white, 2 teaspoons water, and the vanilla until foamy. Add the pecans and stir so they are well coated with egg white.

3. Working quickly, add the sugar, salt, cinnamon, and nutmeg, and toss well to coat. Immediately spread the sugary pecans onto the prepared baking sheet. You want to work fast to try to prevent the sugar from completely dissolving in the egg white.

4. Bake the pecans for 30 minutes, stirring and turning them occasionally, until they are browned, toasted, and completely dry, no longer wet from egg white. Cool them completely and break any clusters into individual nuts if necessary. Store the nuts in an airtight container at room temperature for up to 2 weeks.

Holiday Peppermints

Real peppermint oil gives the clearest, strongest flavor, but milder peppermint extract is perfectly fine. You can also try coconut, orange, or lemon extract instead, and vary the colors as you prefer. Boiling sugar is an adults-only job, but let kids dust on the confectioners' sugar and crack the finished candy. A bag of homemade, jewel-toned suckable sweets is a terrific gift.

2 cups sugar

¾ cup light corn syrup

1 teaspoon pure peppermint oil (or 2 teaspoons peppermint extract)

4 drops red or green food coloring

Confectioners' sugar

1. Lightly butter a rimmed baking sheet. In a heavy-bottomed saucepan over medium heat, combine the granulated sugar, corn syrup, and ½ cup water and stir until the sugar dissolves. Continue to cook, without stirring, until the mixture reaches 300°F (hard-crack stage).

2. Remove the saucepan from the heat and add the peppermint oil and food coloring. Stir with a wooden spoon to combine, then quickly pour the mixture onto the center of the baking sheet. It will spread into a wide pool.

3. Lightly dust the mixture with confectioners' sugar before it is fully set, then let it cool completely. Lift the hardened sheet of candy and give it a sharp crack on the baking sheet to break it into bite-size pieces. Toss the candy with a little additional confectioners' sugar to coat the pieces and prevent them from sticking together. Store them in an airtight tin at room temperature. As long as they stay dry, they'll keep indefinitely.

Homemade Peppermint Patties

I am always disappointed that commercial peppermint patties aren't mintier. I like a stronger contrast between the creamy filling and the bite of strong mint, set off by dark chocolate, so I use a good dose of pure peppermint oil when I make them at home. You can adjust the amount to taste, but this is one recipe where it's best to find the real thing and not settle for peppermint extract, which is much milder. Most gourmet groceries or specialty baking stores have real peppermint oil—or wintergreen is a particularly nice alternative. I also don't mess around with chocolate chips when I make these, instead going for a couple of potent dark bars, such as Ghirardelli's, but you can use 2 cups of chips, if you like.

2 cups confectioners' sugar

2 tablespoons butter, softened

2 tablespoons heavy cream

½ teaspoon pure peppermint oil or 1 teaspoon peppermint extract

12 ounces dark chocolate (such as Ghirardelli's 60% or 70% cacao bars)

1 tablespoon vegetable oil or solid vegetable shortening

1. In a stand mixer or with a hand mixer on low, blend together the sugar, butter, cream, and peppermint oil. When combined, increase the speed to medium and beat for 2 to 3 minutes, until thick and creamy. Chill the fondant for 1 to 2 hours in the refrigerator, until it's firm enough to hold its shape.

2. Line a baking sheet with wax or parchment paper. Roll heaping teaspoons of the peppermint fondant into balls about 1 inch in diameter and lay them on the prepared baking sheet 2 inches apart. With the bottom of a glass, press each ball into a flat disc; apply gentle pressure to try to make each one an even circle with smooth edges. If the edges crack, pinch and mold them back together. Chill the fondant circles for 30 minutes while you prepare the chocolate.

3. Break up the chocolate and melt it with the oil or shortening in the top of a double boiler over simmering water, stirring frequently. When the chocolate is smooth, remove the mint discs from the refrigerator and use 2 forks to dip them into the chocolate, lifting the patties with the forks underneath rather than piercing the surface. The tines of the forks will let the excess drip off before you lay the coated patties back on the parchment or wax paper.

4. When they're all dipped, chill the mints until they're solid, about 30 minutes, then pack them in an airtight container in layers separated by parchment or wax paper and store them for up to 2 weeks in the refrigerator.

Pamelas

an Old South tradition: homemade candied orange peel in chocolate *Makes about 1 pound candy*

I love plain chocolate, I love chocolate and mint, but what I really love is chocolate and orange, and this classic candy features the two, alone in unabashed love. Kids may not love to eat these quite as much as adults do, but they love making them! Don't buy hefty navel oranges with thick peel. Look for smaller varieties, such as Valencias, with a thinner, more flavorful rind, and scrub the exteriors well (and, ideally, start with organic oranges).

4 oranges

3 cups sugar

8 ounces dark chocolate (such as Ghirardelli's 60% or 70% cacao bars)

1 tablespoon vegetable oil or solid vegetable shortening

1. Lay an orange on a clean cutting board, then slice off and discard the top and bottom. Cut the orange into quarters, top to bottom, and then carefully slice the rind away from the fruit. Trim and discard any bitter white pith that you see. Repeat with the other 3 oranges, gathering the rind in one bowl and putting the fruit in another, to eat or make into juice (the kids can eat or drink it while you work).

2. Trim the pieces of peel into strips about ¼ inch wide. Place them in a large saucepan and cover them with water. Bring to a boil over high heat and cook for 20 minutes. Drain the pan, discarding the water, then add fresh water and boil again for 20 minutes. Drain.

3. Put the peel back in the pot with 2 cups of sugar and 2 cups of water. Bring the mixture to a boil, stirring to dissolve the sugar, then reduce the heat and simmer gently for 1 hour, stirring now and then. The peel will be tender and almost translucent.

4. Using a slotted spoon, lift the peels out of the syrup and transfer them to a cooling rack set over a rimmed baking sheet. Separate the peels and lay them in rows, then leave them to dry for 1 hour. When they are still slightly tacky to the touch, place the remaining 1 cup sugar in a large bowl and gently add in the peels. Toss them carefully to coat, then return them to the drying rack, shaking off the excess sugar, and leave them to dry completely, uncovered, overnight.

5. When you're ready to dip, break up the chocolate and melt it with the oil or shortening in the top of a double boiler over simmering water, stirring frequently. Line a baking sheet with wax or parchment paper. When the chocolate is smooth, dip each of the strips halfway into the melted chocolate and lay them on the prepared baking sheet to firm up (you may need to chill them for 30 minutes). When they're set, pack them in an airtight container in layers separated by wax paper and store them in the refrigerator for up to 2 weeks.

CHAPTER TWO

Deck the Halls

Ornaments and Decorations

Not all holiday cooking is to eat. Some projects are simply fun to make and display. This chapter is a mix of the delicious and the delightful to behold. Some, like the Stained-Glass Cookies, can decorate a tree or window for a few days before you allow kids to eat them. Others, such as the Applesauce and Cinnamon Ornaments, include glue and lots of spices, so they were never meant to be edible, but they will remain fragrant and festive for several years to come. Don't be shy about letting your kids make these decorations, with all the mess and hullaballoo that entails. I find that the things I treasure most as the years go by are the things I let them do by themselves, rather than insisting that something had to be rolled just so or made with a particular cookie cutter. I love finding their fingerprints and whimsical notions imprinted on each item. If I want something done a certain way—well, that's *my* ornament. The kids can make their own!

Some kitchen projects are a little more elaborate, maybe a little more special, than others, and I think of them more as entertainment than as cooking. It's a way for the family to spend low-key time together at very little expense, and the result is either extremely tasty, beautiful to look at, or, ideally, both.

What I love about making something like the Bûche de Noël with my kids is that they still get so excited about it. Chocolate cake! That you fill with whipped cream and roll up! That looks like a *log*! When we made the Cream Puff Christmas Tree—a mountain of cream puffs stuck together with icing and drizzled with chocolate—they nearly burst from delight, and frankly, I was pretty excited myself. The kids' thrill makes the project a pleasure for us parents, and then we all get a lovely dessert. Really, what more can you ask from a recipe? Christmas is in the air, and something beautiful, homemade, and sweet is on the dining room table!

Endless Candy Garlands

Makes as many feet of garland as you have candy, line, and patience

These are so simple to make and kids love them so much that they are well worth the fuss of finding fishing line and large plastic needles. If your child has ever been given any sort of kid-friendly embroidery or needlepoint set (for some reason, both my boys love these and have several), you may well have a plastic needle sitting around. Otherwise, large plastic needles or large, child-friendly metal needles with a big eye for easy threading are easily found at craft stores. Any fishing line or filament you may find in your household's fishing gear is fair game (ahem); otherwise, look for transparent line in the fishing aisle of any big-box store. In a pinch, use dental floss.

Use red-and-white peppermint pinwheels, or alternate the red ones with the green-and-white type. You can also use multicolored round sourballs—anything that is individually wrapped.

Wrapped hard candies
Transparent fishing line
Large plastic needlepoint needles (one per child)

1. Pull out a 4-foot length of fishing line. Six inches in from one end, tie the line around a wrapped end of one candy. Thread the other end of the fishing line through the eye of the needle and tie a little knot to keep the line threaded.

2. Pull the needle gently through the opposite side of the wrapper. Continue with additional candies, pushing the needle carefully in one end of the wrapped candy (through the actual twist of the wrapper), and then out through the other twist of the wrapper. Be sure to string the candy on loosely, leaving a bit of space between the flared ends of the wrappers so that they're not crushed together. It should look as if the candies are invisibly connected and practically floating on air when you wrap the garland around your Christmas tree or loop it over doorways or mantels.

3. When you reach the end of the string, remove the needle and tie the fishing line off onto the second twisted end of the last wrapper, just as you started the first candy.

4. To make a longer string, follow steps 1 through 3 again. If you like, tie the second garland onto the end of the first. Continue making garlands until you run out of candy or time.

Gumdrop Doorknob Hangers

Little 6-inch wreath forms are super-inexpensive at craft websites such as orientaltrading.com, and they make adorable doorknob hangers. This is perhaps one of the silliest yet most charming ways to decorate your house, and hence a great favorite with children. If you can find smaller wreath forms, by all means buy them, but in my house the 6-inch diameter lets the door open and close undisturbed. I confess that I have railed in print against the dangers of hiding toothpicks in food, where children might bite down on them, and here I am, using toothpicks. But it's one thing to tuck a toothpick into a cupcake topper and quite another, I think, to use it in a craft item, where the base already consists of something inedible. These gumdrop door hangers are not intended to be eaten, and even with the sugar coating on their surface, I have found that they'll stay pretty and pest-free through the holiday season in a dry, warm house. They do get a little picked-over-looking toward the end, when my youngest plucks off gumdrops from the underside for the occasional snack. He's old enough now to know to pull it off the toothpick anchor first.

1 box wooden toothpicks

2 pounds regular-size gumdrops, not the jumbo kind (the wreaths can be multicolored, or make each one a single color)

3 Styrofoam wreath forms, 6 inches in diameter

3 pieces 1-inch-wide velvet or grosgrain ribbon, each 18 inches long

1. Break about 15 toothpicks in half to start (you can break more as you go along). Poke the broken end into the bottom center of a gumdrop and then poke that gumdrop into the wreath. You'll probably find it takes a row of 6 gumdrops to bridge the width of the circle.

2. Continue around the wreath, poking in gumdrops close together to fill in the front and sides (not the back). It looks much better to stagger the rows a bit rather than trying to fill them in using very straight lines.

3. When your wreath form is covered with gumdrops, use a pastry brush (or your fingers) to brush off any sugar on the candy that may have come loose from handling the gumdrops. Loop a ribbon around the top and tie the ribbon into a large bow. Hang this over a doorknob, so that the wreath dangles several inches under the door handle and the bow is on top. Repeat with remaining wreath forms, gumdrops, and ribbons.

Stained-Glass Cookies

Makes about 3 dozen cookies

Crushed candy melts into a little stained-glass window in these delicate little goodies. They're especially beautiful when hung on a miniature tree so that viewers can appreciate the color and design. They won't last all season, since the hard candy windows absorb moisture from the air and will eventually start to disintegrate. Ideally, you can hang them somewhere for a party or event, and then let kids eat them after it's over. It's also fun to hang them on a window, using suction-cup-hangers that can be found at craft stores. Then you really get to see the light shine through your designs.

½ cup (1 stick) butter, softened

1 cup sugar

1 egg

1 teaspoon vanilla extract

Grated zest of 1 lemon

2 cups all-purpose flour

½ teaspoon baking powder

2 cups hard candies, such as Jolly Ranchers, in different colors

18 feet of ¼-inch ribbon (optional)

1. Cream the butter and sugar in a large bowl with an electric mixer until fluffy. Beat in the egg, vanilla, and lemon zest, then add the flour and baking powder. Form the dough into 2 balls, wrap each in plastic, and chill them for 30 minutes.

2. While the dough is chilling, unwrap the candies, dividing them into groups according to color, and put each color in a small zip-top storage bag. Let your kids use the bottom of a heavy mug to crush the candy into tiny pieces (it doesn't have to be powder; little chunks are fine).

3. Preheat the oven to 350°F and line 2 baking sheets with parchment paper.

4. Sprinkle a little flour on a clean work surface and roll out the first ball of dough to ¼ inch thick. Use cookie cutters to cut out holiday shapes and lift the cookies onto the baking sheets with a spatula, leaving 2 inches between each cookie. Use the tip of a paring knife to cut out the interior of each cookie, following the outline but leaving at least ¾ inch of cookie dough as a rim. (You can also just cut a diamond or a circle in the center of the cookie, or you can use another, smaller cookie cutter.) If you want to, use the tip of the paring knife or a drinking straw to cut a little round hole at the top of each cookie, leaving a generous rim of cookie dough above the hole.

5. Use a teaspoon to sprinkle one color of the crushed candy into the opening you've cut out of each cookie. Fill it in evenly, but be careful not to sprinkle the candy on the dough. When all the cookies are filled, put the baking sheets in the refrigerator for 10 minutes. This will stop the cookie dough from spreading so much in the oven.

6. Bake the cookies for 8 minutes, just until the dough is set and the candy is melted. Don't let them get brown, or they won't look as pretty! Let them cool on the baking sheet for 5 minutes. (This is the time to check them to be sure the optional holes for the ribbon are all still open. If not, use the knife or straw to open the hole again while the cookie is still soft.) Transfer the cookies to a cooling rack to cool completely. Repeat with the remaining dough and candy.

7. When all the cookies are cool, thread a thin loop of ribbon through the hole at the top of each and knot the ends together. Repeat with the remaining cookies. The cookies will survive for about 1 week at room temperature.

Gingerbread People

Some gingerbread is a little anemic when it comes to spicing—too much reliance on cinnamon. I like gingerbread super-spicy and flavorful, so this recipe has a hefty dose of ginger (as all gingerbread should) and a lot of cloves, too, which make the cookies smell wonderful coming out of the oven. Use small gingerperson cutters, ideally about 3 inches high, so that you can make thick, stubby little gingerpeople sturdy enough for hanging. These are best to eat after a day or two, when the flavor really blooms. Royal icing dries stiff and hard, and when these cookies dry out completely, they're too hard for anyone but children to enjoy eating, but they can stay on the tree throughout the Christmas season.

FOR THE GINGERBREAD COOKIES:

½ cup (1 stick) butter

½ cup light brown sugar

1 egg

½ cup molasses

1 tablespoon ground ginger

1 ½ teaspoons ground cinnamon

1 teaspoon ground cloves

3 cups all-purpose flour

½ teaspoon baking soda

½ teaspoon baking powder

FOR THE ROYAL ICING:

1 egg white

1 teaspoon lemon juice

1 ½ cups confectioners' sugar

Food coloring, as desired (preferably paste instead of liquid)

1. Cream the butter and brown sugar in a large bowl with an electric mixer until fluffy and then beat in the egg and molasses. Beat in the spices.

2. Sift the flour, baking soda, and baking powder directly into the bowl and mix to make a stiff dough. Divide the dough into 2 discs and wrap each of them in plastic. Chill for at least 1 hour.

3. When you're ready to bake, preheat the oven to 350°F and line 2 baking sheets with parchment paper. Lightly dust a clean work surface with flour, and roll out the first disc to about ¼ inch thick. Cut out gingermen and gingerwomen with cookie cutters or with the tip of a knife. (If you do them freehand, make them stubby without a huge amount of detail.)

4. Lift the cookies onto the prepared baking sheets and use the tip of a knife or a drinking straw to make a hole at the top for hanging, leaving at least a ¼-inch rim of cookie at the top. Refrigerate the full baking sheets for 10 minutes to prevent the cookies from spreading too much when baked.

5. Bake until the cookies are set but not browned, 10 to 12 minutes. Let them cool for several minutes on the baking sheets, then transfer them to a rack to cool completely while you proceed with the remaining dough.

6. When all the cookies are cool, make the royal icing: beat the egg white and lemon juice with an electric mixer until frothy. With the mixer on at medium speed, beat in the confectioners' sugar a little at a time. Then beat on high until it is very thick and glossy, about 3 minutes. Cover the icing with plastic wrap placed directly on the surface until you're ready to use it.

7. To decorate, divide the royal icing into small cups or bowls and color it as desired (paste coloring will give a more intense color than liquid).

8. Put the icing in a pastry bag fitted with a small round tip. (Alternatively, spoon it into a sandwich-size zip-top storage bag. Press out the air and use scissors to cut off a very tiny corner. If the stream is not quite big enough when you begin squeezing out the icing, cut the hole a bit bigger, but use caution—once you've cut it, you can't make it smaller! If it's way too big, pipe the icing right into a second bag and try again.) Pipe a rim around the outside of each cookie (I like white) and let it dry for 10 to 15 minutes at room temperature. Put additional colors in other bags and flood the cookies with color inside the lines you've piped. Let them dry completely before threading a length of narrow ribbon (I like red satin) through the hole at the top of each cookie and hanging it on the tree.

Snow Angels and Stars

A rich chocolate cookie forms the blank canvas for your snowy sugar fantasies. Let the kids make stencils by trimming out snow angels, stars, or snowflakes from slips of paper. Then lay these stencils on the cookie's surface and let the confectioners' sugar snow gently drift down from above. If you want to hang them somewhere, take the cookies out of the oven while they are only half baked, stencil the still-damp dough, and return them to the oven. (If you stencil them before parbaking, the shapes will deform as the cookies spread.) As they finish baking, the sugar will stick. If you're just eating them, though, you can stencil them after baking.

½ cup (1 stick) butter, softened

¾ cup sugar

1 egg

1 teaspoon vanilla extract

1½ cups all-purpose flour

⅓ cup unsweetened cocoa powder

½ teaspoon baking powder

½ teaspoon salt

Confectioners' sugar

1. Preheat the oven to 350°F and generously grease 2 baking sheets. With a mixer, cream the butter and sugar until light and fluffy. Beat in the egg, and then add the vanilla. Stir in the flour, cocoa, baking powder, and salt until combined.

2. Lightly flour a work surface and roll out half the dough to about ¼ inch thick. Cut it into 2-inch squares or rounds (or any shape you prefer). Lift the cookies onto the prepared baking sheets and place them in the freezer for 10 minutes. Bake for about 10 minutes, until the cookies look dry and puffed. Do not let them brown. Cool them on a rack.

3. While the cookies are cooling, cut out several squares of paper just larger than the cookies. Fold each slip of paper in half and cut a snow angel, star, or snowflake shape out of the seam side. When you open the paper, you'll have a symmetrical design.

4. To finish, put some confectioners' sugar in a sieve or flour sifter. Lay either the shape you cut out or the paper square from which it was cut over a cookie and dust generously with the confectioners' sugar. Carefully remove the paper to see your lovely design! Store the cookies between layers of wax paper in an airtight container for up to 1 week.

Cornflake Wreaths

green cornflakes with red licorice bows—yummy!

Old-fashioned wreaths made of a sticky cornflake mixture take on new life when you gussy them up with ribbons and bows made of shiny red licorice string. Butter your hands well before shaping the wreaths— kids love to do this. Let the kids also do the decorating with Red Hots or dragées. You could make these with Rice Krispies if you prefer, but cornflakes look more like holly leaves!

½ cup (1 stick) butter

1 bag marshmallows (approximately 10 ounces, or 40 regular marshmallows, or
    4 cups mini marshmallows)

1 teaspoon vanilla extract

Green food coloring (paste or liquid)

6 cups cornflakes

Red Hots and/or silver dragées

Red licorice string

1. Line 2 baking sheets with wax paper. Melt the butter and marshmallows in a large saucepan over medium-low heat, stirring frequently, until the mixture is smooth.

2. Remove the pan from the heat and blend in the vanilla and food coloring, adding just a bit of color at a time to reach the desired shade. Add cornflakes and blend, stirring and mixing gently until they are all coated. Using a pair of spoons, transfer golf ball–size lumps to the wax paper and use the spoons (or your well-buttered fingers) to open up a hole in the center of each one, shaping a wreath.

3. Press Red Hots and dragées around each wreath to look like holly berries and decorative balls.

4. Tie a length of licorice string into a bow and press it into the base of each wreath. Cool the wreaths completely and store them in airtight tins, with rounds of wax paper between the layers, for up to 1 week.

Applesauce and Cinnamon Ornaments

The first time I heard about these ornaments from a friend, I thought she must have gotten the recipe wrong. Mixing equal quantities of cinnamon and applesauce? Surely that could only result in yucky sludge. But in the interests of experimentation, I duly tried it and found that it gives you something more like stiff Play-Doh, something you can actually let your kids work with. The lovely thing about these ornaments is that they're fragrant and long-lasting. If you wrap them in tissue and store them in an airtight container, they'll emerge the following year still smelling of warm spices. You can also make small shapes, such as little bells or birds, and tie them to the bows of Christmas gifts. I have tinkered with the basic version, adding a hefty dose of ground cloves for the scent and a little glue for sturdiness (they were never edible to begin with). You can buy large amounts of cinnamon inexpensively at dollar stores or in large containers at big-box stores. I let my kids shape and cut out what they like, rather than insisting that they use cookie cutters to make specific shapes. The stuff that means the most as the years go by is the stuff they made with their own grubby little hands—it reflects their personalities.

> 2 cups ground cinnamon
> 1½ cups applesauce (smooth, plain, store-bought)
> 2 tablespoons ground cloves
> 2 tablespoons white school glue
> 6 feet of ¼-inch ribbon (optional)

1. Blend all the ingredients in a bowl, using a spoon to start, and then your hands, kneading to work it to a pliable dough.

2. Turn the mixture out onto a clean work surface (you can dust it with a little additional cinnamon if needed—flour would discolor the ornaments) and roll it out to about ½ or ¼ inch thick.

3. Use cookie cutters or the tip of a paring knife to cut out any holiday shapes you like. Lay them flat on a baking sheet lined with wax paper and use a paring knife or drinking straw to make a little ¼-inch hole in each, so a ribbon can be attached for hanging.

4. Allow the ornaments to sit for 3 to 4 days at room temperature, until they are completely dry and stiff. Thread a narrow ribbon (I like red satin) through the little hole in each one, and hang it on the tree or tie it on a gift box, as desired. Do not eat!

Christmas Tree Ornament Cookies with Cookie Paint

don't eat them all before they go on the tree

Makes 2 to 3 dozen cookies

Bright cookie paint will beguile many a child on a long winter's afternoon. You've never seen your little artists bloom like they will when you provide cookie canvases and sugary "paint." You can use any cookies, such as the gingerbread cookies pictured here (recipe on page 44), but the bright paint is especially pretty on a sugar cookie. You don't even need cookie cutters to shape this easy-to-handle sugar cookie dough into circles or diamonds. You can use the tip of a paring knife to make any shape you like or use the rim of a glass, if you like a more uniform look. Paste food coloring, rather than liquid, will give a much more intense color.

FOR THE COOKIES:
1 cup (2 sticks) butter, softened
1½ cups confectioners' sugar
1 tablespoon vanilla extract
1 egg
2¼ cups all-purpose flour
½ teaspoon baking powder

FOR THE COOKIE PAINT:
1 tablespoon butter, softened
2 cups confectioners' sugar
3 tablespoons milk
½ teaspoon vanilla extract
Food coloring, preferably paste
Approximately 18 feet of ¼-inch ribbon

1. Cream the butter and sugar in a large bowl with an electric mixer until smooth, then beat in the vanilla and egg.

2. Mix the flour and baking powder, then blend them into the butter mixture. Wrap the dough in plastic and chill it for 30 minutes.

3. Preheat the oven to 350°F and lightly grease a baking sheet. Roll half the dough to ¼ inch thick on a lightly floured surface and use cookie cutters or the rim of a glass to make large circles.

4. Lift the cookies onto the baking sheet with a spatula. Use a paring knife or drinking straw to make a hole in the top of each about ½ inch from the edge. Bake the cookies for about 8 minutes, until they are just set and not at all browned. Cool them completely on the baking sheet.

5. To decorate, use a stand or hand mixer to blend all the cookie paint ingredients except the food coloring. Divide the icing into small bowls and tint them with food coloring to make any colors you like. Use clean small paintbrushes to smooth icing on the cookies (you can also simply use a knife or the back of a spoon to smear on one color). If you're using more than one color on a cookie, apply the paint thinly and let each color dry a little while before adding the next.

6. When all the cookies are dry, thread thin loops of ribbon through the hole at the top of each and knot the ends together. Repeat with the remaining cookies.

Teddy Bear Countdown Calendar

the suspense is just about un-bear-able

Makes 1 calendar

I had three siblings, so when I was a child, there was always a great deal of uproar over whose turn it was to open the little windows on our annual Advent calendar. Inside would be a little knickknack—a tiny plastic toy, sometimes a piece of candy—and we all jealously claimed our turn to get whatever was inside. The final day would reveal a little baby Jesus. However you celebrate your holiday, children love the excitement of a calendar that lets them count down the days to Christmas. The cookies are wrapped in homemade envelopes and pegged to a cheery ribbon strung across a mantel, shelf, or wall. (Each day after the child takes down an envelope with a cookie in it, you can, if you like, replace it with a Christmas card.)

You can use any shape of holiday cookie cutter and pack multiple cookies in each day's envelope for multiple children, if you wish. At my house we like a teddy bear shape, leading up to an actual tiny teddy bear (or some other tiny item or toy) on the final day, and we put fun animal cutouts on the outsides of the envelopes.

- 24 sheets of construction paper
- 8 feet of ½-inch ribbon or cord
- 24 bear-shaped painted cookies (use Christmas Tree Ornament Cookies with Cookie Paint, page 50)
- 25 mini clothes-pegs
- 1 small stuffed teddy bear or other toy
- 1 sheet tissue paper or small brown paper bag

1. Fold the construction paper into envelopes and decorate them as you wish, numbering them 1 to 24.

2. Fasten the long length of ribbon where you want it (the mantel is nice, or string it across a bookshelf the kids can reach), using thumbtacks or removable tape. Secure it in several places, so it can bear the weight of the cookies.

3. Wrap each cookie in plastic wrap, slip it in an envelope, and tape the envelope shut. Use clothes-pegs to clip the envelopes to the ribbon you've strung up.

4. Wrap the real teddy bear or toy in tissue paper or a brown paper bag, write "Do not open till Christmas!" on it, and clip it at the end of the line. Each day, let a child take off a cookie. (The cookies may be a little dry toward the end of the month, but your child won't care.)

White and Dark Chocolate Christmas Tree Bars

reverse the centers for oh-so-cute treats *Makes 32 bars*

You have to bake two batches of bars to make these adorable cutouts, but it's no hardship. If you have two identical square baking pans, you can do it at the same time, but it's just as easy to make one batch, mix up the other while the first bakes, then bake the second batch. You don't even have to wash the saucepan in between batches. The crucial piece of equipment here is a tiny Christmas-themed cookie cutter, something 1 to 1½ inches tall. I like my tiny Christmas tree, but you could use stars or candy canes or bells—even little circles would work here. The colder the bars are, the better for cutting them out; that way the edges will remain stiff when you press the white chocolate centers into the dark brownies and vice versa. You'll be the star of the holiday bake sale.

FOR THE WHITE CHOCOLATE BLONDIES:
½ cup (1 stick) butter
4 ounces white chocolate (such as Ghirardelli's White Chocolate Baking Bar)
¾ cup light brown sugar
1 teaspoon vanilla extract
2 eggs
⅔ cup all-purpose flour

FOR THE DARK CHOCOLATE BROWNIES:
½ cup (1 stick) butter
4 ounces semisweet chocolate (such as Ghirardelli's 60% or 70% cacao bar)
¾ cup sugar
1 teaspoon vanilla extract
2 eggs
⅔ cup all-purpose flour

1. Preheat the oven to 350°F and line an 8-inch square metal baking pan with parchment paper, letting 2 inches hang over the pan at either side.

2. Prepare the blondies first: Put the butter in a large saucepan over medium heat. Break the chocolate bar into squares and put them in the butter. Heat over medium-low heat, stirring frequently, until the chocolate has nearly melted. Remove the pan from the heat and let the mixture sit for several minutes, stirring now and then, until it's smooth.

3. Working in the saucepan, stir in the brown sugar and vanilla, then beat in the eggs. Fold in the flour, stirring just until mixed, being careful not to overmix. Pour the batter into the prepared pan and bake for 25 to 30 minutes, until the blondies are set in the center and a tester comes

out clean. Let the bars cool for 5 minutes in the pan, then lift them out using the parchment overhang, and set them on a wire rack to cool.

4. Line the pan again with parchment and repeat steps 1 through 3 with the ingredients for the brownies. There's no need to wash the saucepan in between batches. (That's why you started with the white chocolate!)

5. Once the blondies and brownies have cooled to room temperature, transfer them to a cutting board and cut each panful into sixteen 2-inch squares. Put all the squares in the freezer for an hour or so, until they're chilled and very firm.

6. Use a tiny cookie cutter to cut the same shape out of the center of all the bars, then gently press the brownie cutouts into the centers of the blondies and the blondie cutouts into the centers of the brownies. Transfer the bars gently to an airtight container, placing sheets of wax paper between layers, and store them at room temperature for up to 1 week.

Bûche de Noël

the holiday Yule log—to eat, not burn

As a young baker, I found the idea of a bûche de Noël *(literally, a "Christmas log") intimidating. It had a French name, to start, and cookbooks always showed it decorated with mushrooms made of meringue. It seemed fussy and difficult. On the other hand, I took keenly to jelly rolls. What do you know? A* bûche de Noël *is nothing more than a chocolate jelly roll with chocolate whipped cream. It's a dream to throw together, and you do* not *need meringue mushrooms. The classic presentation is to cut off the end of the roll and stick it to top of the cake, like the stump of a branch that was cut off the trunk, and to drag a fork through the whipped cream to make wavy lines like tree bark, but it's not necessary. You can just dust the whole thing with some confectioners' sugar "snow."*

4 ounces semisweet chocolate (such as Ghirardelli's 60% cacao bar)

6 eggs, separated

1 teaspoon cream of tartar

1/3 cup plus 1/4 cup sugar

2 teaspoons vanilla extract

Confectioners' sugar

1/4 cup unsweetened cocoa powder

2 cups heavy cream

1. Preheat the oven to 350°F and lightly grease a rimmed 17-by-12-inch baking sheet (also known as a jelly-roll pan). Then line the pan with parchment or wax paper.

2. Break up the chocolate into a microwavable bowl and heat it for 1 minute on high. Stir vigorously. If it needs more time to melt, microwave it in 10-second bursts, stirring after each, and giving it a few moments to continue melting. When the chocolate is smooth, set it aside to cool slightly.

3. Using an electric mixer, beat the egg whites with the cream of tartar until stiff but not dry.

4. In another bowl, using the same beaters, beat the egg yolks with 1/3 cup sugar and 1 teaspoon vanilla until the mixture is thick and much paler. This will take 4 to 5 minutes. Mix in the melted chocolate, then gently fold in the egg whites. Spread the batter into the pan and bake for 15 minutes, until just set. Cool slightly.

5. Lay out a clean dish towel on a work surface and sift confectioners' sugar over it generously, all the way to the edges. Turn the cake top-side down onto the surface of the sugary towel and gently peel off the wax paper, working slowly so as not to tear the cake. Starting at a short end, roll the towel and cake up together very carefully. The sugar prevents sticking, and the towel helps the cooling cake hold its shape.

6. Wash the beaters. Put the remaining 1/4 cup sugar and the cocoa into a clean bowl and stir. Add 1/4 cup of the cream and beat to combine, making sure there are no lumps. Add the rest of the cream and the remaining 1 teaspoon vanilla, and beat until the cream forms soft peaks.

7. Unroll the cake gently and spread 1½ cups of the whipped cream over the surface, spreading it out to the edges. Roll the cake up again, this time without using the towel, and transfer it carefully to a serving platter, seam-side down. (It's okay if it cracks. The whipped cream will cover it.)

8. Use the remaining whipped cream to frost the sides of the cake but not the ends. If you like, cut a 3-inch slice diagonally off one end and press it against the side of the cake, like a forked piece of wood on the side of a log. Use a knife to smooth the chocolate whipped cream, and then drag a fork all over the surface of the cream to make lines like bark if you like. Sift a light snow shower of confectioners' sugar over the top, and chill the cake up to 2 days until you are ready to serve it.

Cream Puff Christmas Tree

Makes about 60 small cream puffs, 10 to 12 servings

A proper French croquembouche *is a glorious confection, made of delicate cream puffs piled high and held together with gossamer threads of spun sugar. This is not a* croquembouche. *Cream puffs are a little more complicated than, say, chocolate chip cookies, but this one is so easy. You do beat eggs into a hot batter to make a choux pastry that puffs nicely in the oven, but this simplified version skips piping the batter in favor of dropping it from a teaspoon. Then you fill each puff with whipped cream, pile the puffs up with a little frosting, and finish the whole thing off with a garland of chocolate ganache.*

FOR THE CREAM PUFFS:

10 tablespoons (1 ¼ sticks) butter
1 ¼ cups all-purpose flour
5 eggs

FOR THE FILLING:

2 ½ cups whipping cream
¼ cup sugar
1 ½ teaspoons vanilla extract

FOR THE ICING:

¼ cup (½ stick) butter, softened
3 cups confectioners' sugar
1 teaspoon vanilla extract
1 to 2 tablespoons milk

FOR THE CHOCOLATE DRIZZLE:

½ cup heavy cream
4 ounces dark chocolate (such as Ghirardelli's 60% or 70% cacao bar)

1. Preheat the oven to 400°F and butter 2 baking sheets.

2. To make the cream puffs: Put 1 ¼ cups of water and the butter in a large, heavy saucepan over medium heat and bring it to a rolling boil. Using a wooden spoon, stir in the flour until smooth. Take the pan off the heat and cool for 5 minutes, stirring a few times. Break in the eggs, one at a time, beating vigorously after each. Continue to beat until the mixture is shiny and pulls away from the sides of the pan. (You can also do this with a stand mixer.)

continued

3. Use a pair of spoons to drop the batter by the teaspoon onto the prepared pans. Don't crowd the pastry; about 1 dozen puffs per sheet is good. Bake, in batches, for 25 to 30 minutes, until they are puffed and golden. Lift the puffs onto racks and cool them completely.

4. While the puffs cool, make the filling: Whip the cream with the sugar and vanilla until soft peaks form.

5. Then, make the icing: Beat the butter until fluffy, then gradually beat in the confectioners' sugar. Add the vanilla and beat in the milk by the teaspoon, adding only as much as needed to make a stiff frosting. This is your glue, so don't make it too thin.

6. Pile the whipped cream into a large pastry bag fitted with a large round tip. Use a paring knife to cut a hole in the side of each cream puff. Insert the tip of the pastry bag and pipe a little whipped cream into each puff. (A pastry bag is easy here, but you can also split the puffs, fill them, and push them back together.)

7. Set aside the prettiest cream puff for the top of your tree. Pick out the largest puffs and spread a bit of icing on the base of each one. Arrange them into an 8- or 9-inch circle (using 15 to 18 puffs) on a serving platter. Add a second, smaller layer, spreading a bit of icing on the base of each to stick them to the ones below. Continue in this manner, building a cone shape and ending with the reserved puff on top. Refrigerate the cream puff tree for up to 3 hours.

8. When ready to serve, make the chocolate drizzle: Bring the cream nearly to a boil in a small saucepan. Remove it from the heat. Break the chocolate into the cream and stir to melt it. Whisk until the mixture is smooth. Right before serving, drizzle chocolate sauce from a spoon over the outside of the cream puff tree. Serve extra chocolate sauce on the side.

Popcorn and Cranberry Garlands

old-fashioned and lovely to look at   *Makes as many feet of garland as you have materials*

As a kid, I yearned for a needle and lots of thread so I could make popcorn and cranberry strings at Christmas; I must have read about it in a Laura Ingalls Wilder story or somewhere equally quaint. My own mother thought it was messy—all that popcorn everywhere!—and dangerous—needles?!—so of course her resistance cemented my desire. When I first joyfully proposed it to my own kids they were completely disinterested. Nowadays, their little digitally altered attention spans make them less inclined to spend hours on end threading popcorn and cranberries on strings, but I solve that problem by presenting it as a contest, with a prize for the kid who makes the longest garland. And I use large plastic needles, dental floss or fishing line instead of thread, and dried cranberries instead of fresh ones, (which sag and rot): All a big improvement on the old days.

> Large plastic embroidery needles (one per child)
> Dental floss or transparent fishing line
> Air-popped popcorn (not microwave popcorn, which is too greasy)
> Dried cranberries

1. Thread a 4-foot length of floss or line onto a needle and tie it in a knot just below the eye of the needle.

2. At the other end of the line, about 6 inches from the end, tie the floss or line around a piece of popcorn or a cranberry to make an anchor.

3. Start threading either popcorn or cranberry on each line, but not both! They don't mix well, but two garlands can be hung side by side, or tied end to end.

4. When you're 6 inches from the end of the line, wrap it around the final piece of popcorn or cranberry and tie it off. Repeat until you've made as many garlands as you want.

5. The garlands can be attached to one another in any combination; you may wish to alternate stretches of popcorn and cranberry. They will last 2 to 3 weeks, though they are inclined to look a little shrunken toward the end.

Candy Cane Twists

Makes about 3 dozen cookies

I like to put a little peppermint flavoring into the sweet dough for these candy cane cookies, but you can skip that and just add vanilla instead. Either way, you'll get a beautifully tender sugar cookie—thanks to all that cream cheese—that's even better when twisted into a candy cane shape. Chill the dough well before handling for best results, and if it's just too difficult to twist two colors together, let your kids shape them into individual red-and-white canes—they're still just as fun.

4 ounces cream cheese, softened

½ cup (1 stick) butter, softened

1 cup confectioners' sugar

1 egg

1 teaspoon vanilla extract

1 teaspoon pure peppermint extract (or ¼ teaspoon peppermint oil)

2½ cups all-purpose flour

½ teaspoon baking powder

½ teaspoon salt

Red food coloring paste

½ cup hard peppermint candies, or 5 to 6 mini candy canes, unwrapped

1. In a large bowl, beat the cream cheese, butter, and sugar with an electric mixer until fluffy. Beat in the egg, vanilla, and peppermint extract. Stir in the flour, baking powder, and salt. Take half the dough out of the bowl, set it on a sheet of plastic wrap, form it into a disc, and wrap it in the plastic. Blend the red food coloring into the dough remaining in the bowl. Shape the red dough into a disc, then wrap it in plastic. Refrigerate both pieces of dough for at least 2 hours, or overnight.

2. When you're ready to bake the cookies, preheat the oven to 375°F and grease 2 cookie sheets. Put the unwrapped peppermints in a zip-top storage bag and crush them into a fine powder with the bottom of a heavy mug.

3. On a clean work surface, pinch 1 teaspoon of dough off both the white and the red discs, and roll each piece into a 6- to 8-inch snake. Lay the red and white snakes side by side and then twist them gently together. Place the twist on the baking sheet and curve it like a candy cane. Sprinkle it with the crushed peppermints. Repeat with the remaining dough. If the dough gets too warm while you are working, return the discs to the refrigerator for a few minutes.

4. Bake the twists for 8 to 9 minutes, until they just begin to firm up. Don't let them brown. Transfer the cookies to a wire rack to cool completely.

Snow Cream

If you ate this as a kid, you'll recognize the flavor immediately. There's hardly a child anywhere who doesn't go wild with excitement over a bowl of ice cream made out of snow. You might want to supervise the snow collecting to make sure it's clean and white, but once you're all back inside, let your child stir in the sugar and vanilla and pour the creamy milk over his or her own bowl of snow. The mixing is half the fun!

¼ to ½ cup whole milk

1 to 2 tablespoons sugar (or to taste)

½ teaspoon vanilla extract

1½ cups (more or less) clean, fresh snow

1. In a small jug, mix the milk, sugar, and vanilla.

2. Fill a serving bowl with the fresh snow.

3. Pour the sweetened milk over the snow, stirring to combine. Some people like their snow cream stiff and snowy; others like it slushy and milky. How the snow cream turns out will also depend on whether the snow is light and fluffy or heavy and slushy. Pour on as much sweetened milk as looks good to you. Take the time to experiment to make the snow cream taste right. Your kids will remember the taste forever.

Christmas Cupcake Balls page 74

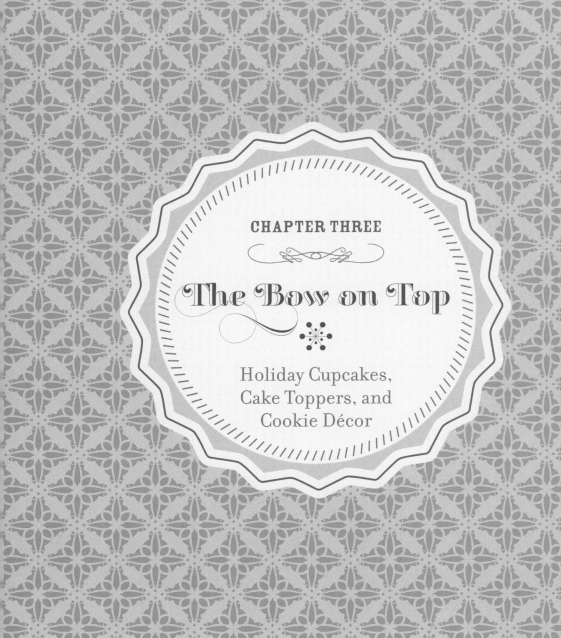

CHAPTER THREE

The Bow on Top

❋

Holiday Cupcakes,
Cake Toppers, and
Cookie Décor

Kids never get tired of fun, decorative food, but while they'll *ooh* and *ahh* at a stack of cream puffs shaped into a tree (page 59), they really get excited about treats on a slightly smaller scale—like any cupcake or cookie.

That's why the tasty goodies in this chapter are perfect for children's holiday parties and school events. They're also great for entertaining little ones at family gatherings. Set all the children in the house around the kitchen table with enough chocolate dough to make Santa Mice (page 77), or give them the pieces to fashion their own reindeer on top of a cupcake. Little fingers are surprisingly adept at decorating, so if you find that you're having a hard time making your own cupcake ornament balls look round and smooth or you can't get Frosty's candy-corn nose to sit right in his miniature-cupcake face, look around for the nearest pair of willing little hands. Even if the final product isn't perfect, your child's happiness will be complete.

Shortbread Holiday Boxes

pipe on a bow made out of icing   *Makes about 1½ dozen shortbreads*

Cookie doughs with lots of butter—such as shortbread, with its two-to-one ratio of flour to butter—are very forgiving. They don't rise too much and generally keep their shape, so you can mold them all sorts of ways. That means you can treat a stiff shortbread dough sort of like Play-Doh and mold it into any shape you want. It's best to keep the shapes relatively small: too big, and they'll crack before they bake through. I like to make 1-inch cubes that are just big enough for me to pipe on a red ribbon and bow of icing. A plate of them looks like a mound of wrapped gifts under a Christmas tree.

Normally, I'm opposed to using store-bought icing, but those ready-colored tubes of decorating icing—not the gel, but the buttercream style—are just right for this. Use any color you like and decorate away.

1½ cups (3 sticks) butter, softened

⅔ cup confectioners' sugar

1½ teaspoons vanilla extract

3 cups all-purpose flour

1 recipe Royal Icing (page 44)

1 tube (4.25 ounces) decorating icing

1. Using an electric mixer, beat the butter and confectioners' sugar in a large bowl until creamy. Stir in the vanilla. Mix in the flour, then shape the dough into a disc and wrap it in plastic. Chill it for at least 1 hour.

2. When you're ready to bake, preheat the oven to 350°F and line a baking sheet with parchment paper. Mold the dough into 1-inch cubes, using your fingers to smooth the sides and pinch the edges sharp. Arrange the boxes on the baking sheet and bake for 10 minutes, until they are just lightly golden. Don't overbake.

3. Let the cookies cool completely, then spoon royal icing over each box, letting it drip down and dry. Use the tube of decorating icing to pipe a ribbon up one side, then across and down the opposite side. Turn the cookie and repeat. Finish with a few loops of icing on top to look like a bow. (You can use real ribbon if you prefer.) These are better served at once; otherwise, pack them in a single layer in a shallow container.

Snowman Cupcakes

ohhh, Frosty the cakeman . . .

Making a foolproof cupcake recipe with your kids is a good way to spend a snowy afternoon. Turning those cupcakes into sugary snowmen is an even better one. You can use decorating gel instead of candy to create the snowmen's faces, if you like. The fruit-leather accessories are optional! For a more formal topper, use a bit of icing to stick a Reese's Mini upside down onto a chocolate cookie for a dashing hat.

FOR THE CUPCAKES:

½ cup (1 stick) butter, softened

½ cup sugar

2 eggs

1 teaspoon vanilla extract

1½ cups all-purpose flour

1½ teaspoons baking powder

½ teaspoon salt

½ cup milk

FOR THE FROSTING:

½ cup (1 stick) butter, softened

1 pound (about 4 cups) confectioners' sugar

1 teaspoon vanilla extract

3 tablespoons milk

TO DECORATE:

Assorted small candies such as Red Hots, sprinkles, and candy corn

Fruit leather

1. Preheat the oven to 350°F. Line 6 regular-size muffin cups with cupcake liners, and line 6 mini muffin cups with mini liners.

2. Using an electric mixer, cream the butter and sugar in a large bowl until light. Add the eggs and vanilla, and beat for 3 to 4 minutes, until the batter is creamy and fluffy.

3. Add 1 cup of the flour along with the baking powder and salt, and mix to combine. Add all the milk and mix until combined, then add the remaining flour and stir it in completely. Spoon the batter into the cupcake liners.

4. Bake the cupcakes for about 15 minutes, until a skewer poked into the center of a mini cupcake comes out clean. Remove the minis and let the larger ones bake another 4 or 5 minutes, until a skewer comes out clean. Cool the cakes completely on a rack.

5. Combine the frosting ingredients and beat the mixture until it's smooth; spread it on the larger cupcakes.

6. To assemble the snowmen, make the face by putting an unwrapped mini cupcake on its side on top of a larger cupcake and pipe frosting onto it to cover. Shape the eyes, nose, and mouth with candy (candy corn makes a good nose, if you have any). Use fruit leather cut into strips to make a scarf.

Coconut Rice Krispie Snowmen

Rice Krispie treats find a whole new life as a moldable material to make kid-friendly shapes. You have to monitor the temperature by poking the mixture with a finger to see if it's cool enough to handle. You can mold with greater ease if it is just cool enough for you to touch, but still warm enough to be soft and pliable. If you follow the directions here but substitute two cups of marshmallow cream (or Fluff) in place of the marshmallows, your snowmen will be even whiter.

1 cup shredded coconut

¼ cup (½ stick) butter, plus additional for your hands

1 bag marshmallows (approximately 10 ounces, or 40 regular marshmallows, or 4 cups
   mini marshmallows)

6 cups Rice Krispies cereal

Pretzel sticks

Candy corn

Round candy, such as Red Hots, dragées, or Nerds

Red fruit leather

1. Put the coconut in a shallow bowl. Butter a 9-inch square pan well. Line a baking sheet with wax paper. Melt the butter and marshmallows in a large saucepan over medium-low heat, stirring frequently. Stir in the Rice Krispies and turn the mixture into the prepared pan. (If you leave it in the saucepan while you work, you won't be able to get it out!)

2. Butter your hands and roll spoonfuls of the mixture into small, medium, and large balls. Roll each ball in coconut, then press them together to form snowmen. Set the snowmen on the wax paper.

3. For each snowman, press 2 pretzel arms into the sides of the middle ball. Cut the orange tip off a piece of candy corn and press it into the middle of the face for a nose. Press Red Hots or another round candy up the front to make buttons.

4. Use Nerds or dragées or other small round candies to make eyes and a grin. For the final touch, slice off a strip of fruit leather and wrap it around the snowman's neck for a scarf.

Rudolph Cupcakes

You see various versions of reindeer decorations, but I like those made with a mini vanilla wafer cookie atop a cupcake. Add the obligatory pretzel antlers, some googly marshmallow eyes, and a big red Rudolph nose by way of a red M&M (you can also use a Red Hot, for a smaller, more discreet nose), and you've got a whole herd of reindeer just pawing to get on the move. There are so many little bits to the faces that if you put out some extra candy or cookies or pretzels, kids can entertain themselves for ages playing reindeer games.

¼ cup (½ stick) butter, softened

3 tablespoons unsweetened cocoa powder

1 teaspoon vanilla extract

2½ cups confectioners' sugar

1 to 2 tablespoons milk, if needed

1 dozen store-bought or homemade chocolate cupcakes
   (see Christmas Cupcake Balls, page 74)

12 mini vanilla wafers

12 red M&Ms or Red Hots

12 mini marshmallows

1 tube black decorating gel

24 mini pretzel twists

24 almond slices

1. Make the frosting by using an electric mixer to beat the butter with the cocoa until smooth, then add the vanilla and sugar, beating until combined. If the frosting is stiff, add the milk a little at a time, beating until it's creamy and fluffy. Frost the cupcakes.

2. To decorate a cupcake, lay a mini vanilla wafer, curved-side up, on a cupcake. Use a bit of frosting to glue an M&M low on the protruding part to make the nose.

3. With a pair of kitchen scissors, snip a mini marshmallow in half around the middle. Press the cut sides down into the frosting to make eyes above the wafer. Use a dot of black decorating gel to make pupils in the eyes. The bigger you make the dot and the lower on the eye, the goofier your reindeer will look (presuming you think that's a good thing like I do).

4. Working with a pair of pretzels, break a bit of each pretzel off until it looks antler-shaped and press one into each side. Press an almond slice on the outside of each antler to make ears. Repeat with all the cupcakes.

Snowball Cupcakes

Makes 1 dozen snowballs

Snowball cupcakes are similar to the Christmas Cupcake Balls (page 74), but where those are dolled up with color and glitter galore, these puffy white balls are pure white through and through, from their tender, sour cream cake base to the fluffy cream cheese frosting and coconut flake coating. If you want to keep them as white as possible, do what professional bakers do and get some clear, or white, vanilla from a baking store. Use it for the cake and frosting; even that little hint of brown from the vanilla can keep your snowballs from being as pure as the driven snow (in color, at least)! Sprinkle a little silvery luster sugar on top of each snowball, and you'll swear the sun is glinting off the ice.

FOR THE CUPCAKES:

6 tablespoons (¾ stick) butter, softened

¾ cup sugar

½ teaspoon vanilla extract

2 eggs

1¼ cups all-purpose flour

½ teaspoon baking soda

¼ teaspoon salt

½ cup sour cream

FOR THE FROSTING:

1 package (8 ounces) cream cheese, softened

½ cup (1 stick) butter, softened

Pinch of salt

2 teaspoons vanilla extract

1 pound (about 4 cups) confectioners' sugar

TO FINISH:

4 cups sweetened flaked coconut

Silver or white luster sugar (optional)

1. Preheat the oven to 350°F and line a 12-cup muffin tin with paper liners. (You could simply grease the muffin tin well, since you're going to unwrap each cupcake before decorating, but I find prep and cleanup easier when using the liners!)

2. Cream the butter and sugar in a large bowl using an electric mixer until fluffy, then add the vanilla and beat in the eggs one at a time, mixing well after each.

3. In a small bowl, whisk together the flour, baking soda, and salt. Add half of the flour mixture to the batter, then half of the sour cream. Repeat, mixing just to combine after each addition. Divide the batter between the prepared muffin cups and bake for 20 to 22 minutes, until the tops are just turning golden and the centers spring back when touched with a finger. Place them on a rack to cool.

4. While the cupcakes are cooling, make the frosting: Beat the cream cheese and butter with an electric mixer until creamy, then add the salt and vanilla. Gradually add the confectioners' sugar, mixing until smooth and fluffy.

5. When the cupcakes are completely cool, unwrap them and discard the papers. Frost them generously all over the sides and tops, but not the bottoms.

6. Spread the coconut in a shallow bowl. Working carefully, lift each cupcake from the bottom by sliding a fork or small spatula underneath and tip it into the coconut, upside down. Pat the coconut into the frosted sides so that each cupcake is completely covered. Use the fork or spatula and your fingers to carefully lift the cupcake onto a serving platter. When all the cupcakes have been rolled in the coconut and placed upright again, sprinkle them lightly, if desired, with the luster sugar.

Christmas Cupcake Balls

glittering balls of chocolate cake   *Makes 1 dozen balls*

Luster sugar, also known as glitter sugar, used to be a specialty baking item, but now you can find it in the cake decorating aisle at Walmart—in fact, you can find a lot of one-time rarified cake-decorating items there. You can use plain old not-shiny colored decorating sugar, but the goal is to make the unwrapped cupcakes look like a dozen gleaming holiday ornaments. If you pack them in a cardboard box, the effect is complete. Tuck them into a "nest" of shredded wax paper that you've made by cutting 12-inch squares of wax paper into ¾-inch ribbons.

    6 tablespoons (¾ stick) butter, softened

    ¾ cup sugar

    5 tablespoons unsweetened cocoa powder

    1 teaspoon vanilla extract

    2 eggs

    1 cup all-purpose flour

    ½ teaspoon baking soda

    ¼ teaspoon salt

    ½ cup buttermilk

    1 recipe cream cheese frosting from Snowball Cupcakes (page 72)

    2 or 3 tubes decorating icing in different colors

    Luster and/or glitter sugar

    12 mini marshmallows

    18 inches licorice string

1. Preheat the oven to 350°F and line a 12-cup muffin tin with cupcake papers. (You could simply grease the muffin tin well, since you're going to unwrap each cupcake before decorating, but I find prep and cleanup easier when using the liners!)

2. In a large bowl, cream the butter and sugar until fluffy using an electric mixer. Add the cocoa and vanilla and beat until smooth. Beat in the eggs, one at a time, mixing well after each addition.

3. In a small bowl, whisk together the flour, baking soda, and salt. Add half of the flour mixture to the batter, then half the buttermilk. Repeat with the remaining flour mixture and then the remaining buttermilk. Spoon the batter into the prepared muffin tins and bake for 18 to 22 minutes, until the centers spring back if touched with a finger or a tester comes out with just a few crumbs clinging to it.

4. When the cupcakes are completely cool, unwrap them and discard the papers. Frost each cupcake all over the top and sides, leaving only the bottom unfrosted. Pipe on parallel lines or squiggles of

decorationg icing, and fill in areas between the lines with the decorating sugar. You may want to roll 2 or 3 of the cupcakes wholly in the sugar for a monochromatic look. Use a fork or spatula (and perhaps a careful finger to help balance) to lift the finished cupcakes onto their serving platter or into a box filled with wax paper strips.

5. When the cupcakes are in place, trim the licorice into 12 pieces, each 1½ inches long. Use skewers or a toothpick to make 2 little holes in the top of each marshmallow and fit either end of a length of licorice string into the holes so it looks like a hanging loop. Place one of these marshmallows on each cupcake, setting them at different angles like a group of ornaments jumbled or boxed together.

Chocolate Santa Mice

candy mice with almond ears   *Makes 1 dozen mice*

When I was a child, one of my family's favorite holiday books was Santa Mouse *by Michael Brown, about a little mouse who lives in a lonely, empty house wishing for friends, until one Christmas Eve, Santa whisks him away to be his assistant. I always wondered why Santa happened to have a mouse-size Santa suit, boots, and fake beard, but I guess the old guy is magic. The book was reissued in time for my own children to enjoy it, and now at Christmas they also leave out a little cube of cheese, carefully wrapped in foil, for Santa Mouse to nibble on while Santa enjoys his cookies and milk.*

We like white mice rolled in confectioners' sugar, but if you prefer dusky mice, roll them in ½ cup unsweetened cocoa powder instead.

12 chocolate sandwich cookies or chocolate wafers

6 ounces (1 cup) semisweet chocolate chips

¼ cup sour cream

½ cup confectioners' sugar

24 almond slices

Red or black string licorice, or licorice twists that you can unwind, such as Twizzlers Pull-n-Peel

12 gold or silver dragées

1. Crush the cookies into fine crumbs in a food processor or by placing them in a large, heavy zip-top storage bag and gently beating and rolling them with a rolling pin or bottle.

2. Put the chocolate chips in a microwave-safe bowl and melt the chocolate in the microwave: Heat it on high for 1 minute, then stir well; if you need more time, heat in 10-second bursts, stirring well after each time.

3. Stir in the sour cream and cookie crumbs, and refrigerate the mixture until firm, no longer than 15 to 20 minutes. Do not leave the chocolate in the refrigerator indefinitely; it will become too hard.

4. Line a baking sheet with parchment or wax paper. Butter your hands and roll the chocolate mixture into 12 mouse body shapes—almost ovals, tapered to a point at one end (the nose) and rounded at the other (the tail end). Lay the chocolate shapes on the prepared baking sheet.

5. Place the confectioners' sugar on a plate and roll the mice in it to cover them.

6. Poke holes just above the tapered nose for eyes (your fingernails are perfect for this), and place 2 almond slices behind them at pert angles for ears. Poke a 2- to 3-inch length of licorice into the rounded end for a tail. Add a dragée for a nose. Refrigerate the mice to keep them firm until you serve them. They'll keep in an airtight container in the refrigerator for up to 1 week.

3-D Jigsaw Cookie Ornaments

I'm a big believer in not using cookie cutters. I have plenty of specialty shapes, sure, and they're fun to collect. But as I've said before, there's a reason we use the term "cookie cutter" to describe something that's kind of ordinary, without style or dash. There are very few shapes you can't make yourself by using the tip of a paring knife and a steady hand, and you may be surprised to find how much better a tray of individually cut cookies looks. That said, these stand-up cookies will likely work best for you if you use a cookie cutter! For each cookie, you'll need two of each shape, and if they're identical, they'll balance and stand better. But don't put that paring knife away. You'll be using it to cut slits in each cookie so they will interlock like a puzzle, and then stand upright. You can use a circle cutter and decorate the cookies to look like Christmas tree ornaments, but anything symmetrical will interlock and stand, such as a Christmas tree or snowman shape.

> 1 recipe gingerbread cookie dough (see Gingerbread People, page 44)
> 2 recipes Royal Icing (see Gingerbread People, page 44)
> Food coloring, as desired
> Dragées, small candies, or glitter sugar, as desired

1. Preheat the oven to 350°F and line a baking sheet with parchment paper.

2. Roll a quarter of the dough out on a lightly floured surface to ¼ inch thick. Use a cookie cutter to cut an even number of shapes. Lift them onto the baking sheet and bake for 8 to 10 minutes, until just set but not browned. You want them baked through but not crisp.

3. Let the cookies cool slightly and lift them onto a clean cutting board. Cut a ¼-inch-wide channel that extends about three-quarters of the way up from the bottom of one cookie, then make the same cut down from the top of its mate. Fit the cookies together and see if they'll stand upright. If necessary, separate them and trim a little off the bottom. Depending on the shape, you may also need to trim some of the top off the bottom cookie. Snowmen, for example, may work best if you cut off the head of the bottom cookie, so that only one snowman head rises to the top.

4. Roll, cut, and bake the remaining dough. Separate the cookies, keeping fitted pairs together. Then trim all of the remaining cookies as in Step 3.

5. When all the cookies have been trimmed, decorate! Color the icing as you wish. Add dragées or candy or glitter sugar as desired. When the front decorations of the cookies are entirely dry, you can flip them and repeat the decorating and drying process on the underside, as it will be seen when assembled.

6. When all the decorations are dry, fit the matched pairs together and stand them upright.

Santa's Pack Cookies

a sweet treat hidden inside each one

You know how it's so fun to get a fortune cookie at a Chinese restaurant? The pleasure comes not so much from how good the cookies are—they're usually kind of bland—but in breaking them open to find something, even just that little slip of paper, inside. These cookies are really nothing more than fortune cookies shaped like Santa's pack of toys, with ribbon cinched around the top and a piece of Christmas candy inside. You may feel that peppermint and fortune cookie are flavors best kept separate, but kids won't be so fussy. You can use chocolates—unwrapped mini peanut butter cups, for example—but they'll be inclined to melt when you wrap the hot cookie around them. They'll firm back up as the cookie cools, but be aware that they won't be pristinely beautiful when you break open the cookie.

3 egg whites

½ cup sugar

½ cup (1 stick) butter, melted

1 teaspoon vanilla extract

¼ teaspoon almond extract

3 tablespoons water

1 cup all-purpose flour

18 peppermints or cinnamon hard candies (or any small candies you like), unwrapped

18 pieces of thin red ribbon, each 6 inches long

1. Preheat the oven to 350°F. Line a baking sheet with parchment paper.

2. In a large glass or metal bowl, whip the egg whites and sugar with an electric mixer on high speed until frothy, about 2 minutes. Reduce the speed to low and stir in the melted butter, vanilla, almond extract, water, and flour one at a time, mixing well after each. The batter will be thin, more like pancake batter than cookie dough.

3. Spoon the batter into 4-inch circles on the prepared baking sheets. Leave 2 inches between each cookie to allow for spreading.

4. Bake the cookies for 5 to 7 minutes, until the edges begin to brown slightly. Working quickly, use a spatula to lift a cookie off the sheet and onto a clean work surface. Place a candy in the center and gather the cookie up around it like a beggar's purse, tying a piece of ribbon around the neck of the bag to hold it shut. To help the cookie keep its shape as it cools, you can place it in a muffin tin until it is set. Repeat the process with the remaining cookies.

Meringue Santa Hats

dipped in chocolate and disappearing fast   *Makes 3 dozen meringues*

These crisp, chewy little meringue kisses are so simple, yet so good. Plain, without food coloring or chocolate, they're an addictive treat, but for the holidays, a few drops of red food coloring and a collar of white chocolate make them amusingly reminiscent of little Santa hats. You could instead add a few drops of green coloring, dip them in white or dark chocolate, and call them elf hats. It's the spirit of the thing that your kids will appreciate! When it comes to the dipping, the chocolate isn't hot, and this isn't a particularly messy job, so it's perfect for any small children who may be hanging about. In my house, boys on the cusp of six turned out to be ideal for the project.

> 2 egg whites
> ½ cup sugar
> ½ teaspoon vanilla extract
> Red food coloring, preferably paste
> 1½ cups (9 ounces) white chocolate chips

1. Preheat the oven to 200°F and line a baking sheet with parchment paper or a silicone sheet. (Do *not* use wax paper; it will stick badly! If you don't have the right liners, grease the baking sheet and dust it with flour, shaking off the excess.)

2. In a large glass mixing bowl, beat the egg whites with a hand mixer until soft peaks form. Sprinkle in the sugar, then add the vanilla and a few drops of red food coloring. Go as red as you dare but don't add too much liquid color; paste coloring will make for a more intense final product. Continue beating until the mixture is thick and glossy.

3. Using a teaspoon, drop small dollops of the meringue close together on the baking sheet, lifting the spoon as you drop in order to form a peak on each hat.

4. Bake for 45 minutes, then turn off the oven. Crack the oven door a little to let the heat escape, and let the meringues cool completely in the oven, an hour or so.

5. Put the chocolate in a microwave-safe bowl and microwave it on high for 1 minute. Stir vigorously, then continue to microwave it in 10-second blasts, as necessary, stirring after each, until the chocolate is smooth. Each time you stir, wait a few moments before heating it again; the chocolate may smooth without further cooking. You must be especially careful not to overheat white chocolate chips, or they'll seize into a stiff mass.

6. Dip the base of each meringue in the white chocolate and set it back on a prepared baking sheet. Let the chocolate firm up at room temperature, then store the meringues in an airtight container for 3 or 4 days.

Cranberry Oatmeal
Pecan Cookies page 91

Snow Angels
and Stars page 46

Grandma's Chocolate
Crinkles page 90

CHAPTER FOUR

Cookie Swap

❋

Make It
Easy Again

The initial impulse behind cookie swaps was good:

I'll make a bunch of these, you make a bunch of those, we'll swap and share, and everyone gets a nice variety of Christmas cookies without a lot of fuss.

The result is sometimes more complex than that. People go home disgruntled after they stayed up all night forming delicate tuiles over a rolling pin and all they got in exchange was what look suspiciously like store-bought oatmeal cookies with a dollop of store-bought icing on top. Worse is when baking moms get competitive, and the one person who thought everyone would love her chocolate chip cookies is overwhelmed by the glittering array of petit fours and sandwich cookies.

I propose calling a truce. The best cookie swap I ever attended involved five other moms, a whole bunch of kids (well, ten, but it seemed like more), lots of raw cookie dough, and many bottles of wine. In advance, we all chose a recipe from a roster of simple cookies, made the dough at home, and brought it along to bake together. One of the dads was a musician, and he dropped by to provide accompaniment. So while the kids played and ate cookies, we baked, drank wine, and sang carols all afternoon long. By the end of the day, nobody cared very much how many cookies they went home with, but a terrific time had been had by all, and we still ended up with some holiday baking. That's my idea of a cookie swap.

To that end, every recipe in this chapter makes six dozen, enough to share but not so many as to weary the baker. Three recipes are so easy they don't even require baking, but are still pretty excellent for all that, and one or two are a little fancier for moms who like to show off. They're all designed to make cookie swapping once again the simple pleasure it's meant to be. Don't forget drinks for the grown-ups and a little holiday caroling while you're at it!

Extra-Spicy Gingersnaps

so spicy they'll bite you back

Makes 6 dozen cookies

I think gingerbread and gingersnaps—and ginger ale, for that matter—ought to taste like ginger. So I'm always dubious of recipes that call for something like "½ teaspoon ginger." That's not going to give you a flavor worthy of the name. This recipe calls for a hefty dose of ginger, and the spices are toasted first to bring out the flavor, then heightened with the addition of chopped candied ginger, which you can buy in gourmet stores. If you can't find it, leave it out, or consider adding ½ cup finely chopped candied orange peel (see Pamelas, page 35, to make your own). Since children are usually among my audience when I bake, I never ramp up the heat with black or white pepper. Ginger gives me all the kick I need, and, perhaps surprisingly, kids tend to love these because the spicy flavor is warm and fragrant, not hot. With salted butter and a whole tablespoon of baking soda, the addition of salt to the dough is unnecessary. These cookies are good right out of the oven, but they actually taste better the day after they're made, when the spices really bloom.

1 tablespoon ground ginger

2 teaspoons ground cinnamon

½ teaspoon ground cloves

¾ cup (1½ sticks) butter, softened

1 cup sugar

¾ cup light brown sugar

2 eggs

1 cup molasses

4 cups sifted all-purpose flour

1 tablespoon baking soda

½ cup chopped candied ginger

1. Preheat the oven to 350°F. Grease 2 baking sheets.

2. Put a clean dry skillet over medium heat and add the ginger, cinnamon, and cloves. Shake the pan over the heat for 1 to 2 minutes, just until you smell the spices, then instantly turn the mixture out into a large mixing bowl. If you leave the spices in the hot pan, they may burn.

3. Add the butter and sugars to the bowl with the spices and beat with a mixer until fluffy. Add the eggs and beat to combine, then drizzle in the molasses with the mixer running on low. (It's okay if the mixture seems to separate.) Add the flour and baking soda and mix to combine, then stir in the chopped ginger.

4. Drop the dough by heaping tablespoons onto the baking sheets, leaving 2 inches between each cookie. Bake them for 10 minutes, until just set. Don't overbake them, or they'll get dry—they should still be a little chewy. Repeat with the remaining dough and cool the cookies completely on a rack before storing them in airtight containers for up to 1 week.

Judith's Toffee Thins

My friend Judith Sutton is a wonderful baker and I've been fortunate enough to enjoy many treats from her kitchen, but I had never had these cookies until I found them in her wonderful cookbook, Sweet Gratitude, *which should be in the hands of anyone who likes sugar. I've tinkered ever so slightly with her beautifully simple recipe, but the magic remains. No eggs, no fuss—just mix, roll, slice, bake. The result is like the essence of toffee in a cookie. You can keep a roll of this dough in the freezer for those times when you have low blood sugar and nothing will do but a warm cookie.*

> 1 ½ cups (3 sticks) butter, softened
> 1 ½ cups dark brown sugar
> 1 tablespoon vanilla extract
> 2 ¼ cups all-purpose flour

1. Cream the butter, sugar, and vanilla with an electric mixer until fluffy. Stir in the flour.

2. Divide the dough into three 6-inch-long logs and wrap each in plastic. Chill them for at least 2 hours, or overnight. (The delicate dough needs the long chilling time to be workable.)

3. When you're ready to bake, preheat the oven to 350°F. Use a serrated knife to slice a log into 24 slices, ¼ inch thick, and put them 2 inches apart on baking sheets. Bake for 10 minutes, just until the cookies are golden. Cool them for a few moments on the baking sheet, then transfer them to racks to cool completely. Repeat with the remaining dough. Store the cookies in airtight containers for up to 1 week.

Coconut–Walnut Blondies

Packaged flake coconut is perfectly fine here, but if you ever feel the need to crack a fresh coconut, this is the recipe for using it. Coarsely shredding it on the biggest blade of a shredder gives you a chewier texture in the finished bars and lets the coconut flavor shine through. The additional sugar in packaged flake coconut isn't necessary when you've got so much brown sugar already in the batter. These have an intense, caramel taste that makes them just about the perfect blondie, but I also love them with the addition of a cup (no more) of chocolate chunks, not chips. Then you get a sort of reserved hit of chocolate every bite or two that combines perfectly with the coconut.

    1½ cups (3 sticks) butter
    3 cups light brown sugar
    3 eggs
    1 tablespoon vanilla extract
    1 teaspoon pure almond extract (optional)
    3 cups all-purpose flour
    1½ cups shredded unsweetened coconut
    1½ cups walnut pieces

1. Preheat the oven to 350°F and line the bottom of a 9-by-13-inch pan with foil, leaving a 2-inch overhang at either end. Butter the foil lightly.

2. In a large saucepan, melt the butter over medium heat. Remove it from the heat and stir in the sugar. Add the eggs, vanilla, and almond extract, if you're using it, beating with a wooden spoon to combine.

3. Stir in the flour, coconut, and walnuts, then turn the batter into the prepared pan and bake for 35 minutes, until the blondies are golden on the edges and just set in the center.

4. Cool slightly, then score the top lengthwise to make 6 equal strips and crosswise into 12 sections. Lift the whole piece out with the foil overhang, and when it's cool, cut it into bars along the score marks. Store the blondies in an airtight container for up to 1 week.

Grandma's Chocolate Crinkles

cracked open to show chocolate yumminess inside   *Makes 6 dozen cookies*

You can roll chocolate crinkle cookies in granulated sugar and get a lovely cookie, one that cracks like a gingersnap. Or you can roll the chocolaty dough in confectioners' sugar and get a work of art. This simple version uses cocoa and oil instead of melted chocolate and butter, making them extremely fast to put together. Use regular cocoa or Dutch processed but don't use the "Special Dark" cocoa. It gives the cookies an odd, grayish tinge that takes away from their good looks! If you have some children nearby, set them to rolling the dough and coating it with sugar—it's just the sort of work they like.

4 eggs

1 cup vegetable oil

1½ cups sugar

1½ cups light brown sugar

1 tablespoon vanilla extract

3½ cups all-purpose flour

1 cup unsweetened cocoa powder

1 tablespoon baking powder

1½ teaspoons salt

2 cups confectioners' sugar, or more as needed

1. In a large bowl, beat the eggs and oil with the sugars and vanilla until smooth. Sift the flour, cocoa, baking powder, and salt directly into the bowl and stir to blend. Cover the dough with plastic wrap and chill for 1 hour.

2. When you're ready to bake, preheat the oven to 350°F and line 2 baking sheets with parchment paper. Roll the dough into 1-inch balls and then in the confectioners' sugar, coating them liberally.

3. Place them on the prepared baking sheets, leaving 2 inches between each cookie, and bake for 8 or 9 minutes, until the cookies spread and crackle. Don't overbake them; even if the cookies don't seem quite set in the center, take them out and let them cool. This unusual oil-based dough will get too crispy if you overbake but will set up deliciously chewy once you let the cookies cool completely on a rack.

4. Store the cookies in airtight containers, in layers separated by wax paper, for up to 1 week.

Cranberry Oatmeal Pecan Cookies

chewy rather than crisp   *Makes 6 dozen cookies*

I like oatmeal cookies to be chewy, and this buttery dough does the trick. It also helps to use old-fashioned rolled oats rather than quick-cooking oats. I use only a hint of cinnamon, considering how many cookies this dough makes, but it's just enough to make its presence felt, and it plays nicely off the tart dried cranberries. Adding pecans is overkill, but hey, it's the holidays.

- 1 cup (2 sticks) butter, softened
- 1 cup light brown sugar
- ¾ cup sugar
- 3 eggs
- 2 teaspoons vanilla extract
- 1½ cups all-purpose flour
- 1 teaspoon ground cinnamon
- 1 teaspoon baking soda
- 3 cups old-fashioned rolled oats
- 1½ cups dried cranberries
- 1 cup chopped pecans

1. Preheat the oven to 350°F and grease 2 baking sheets.

2. In a large bowl, cream the butter and sugars with a mixer until light, 3 to 4 minutes. Beat in the eggs and vanilla until fluffy.

3. Add the flour, cinnamon, and soda and mix just to combine, then use a wooden spoon to stir in the oats, cranberries, and pecans.

4. Drop heaping tablespoons of the dough onto the baking sheets, spacing the cookies 2 inches apart. Bake them for 10 minutes, just until the edges are starting to turn golden and the middles are barely firm; don't overbake. Repeat with the remaining dough and let the cookies cool completely on a rack before storing them in an airtight container for up to 1 week.

Dark Chocolate Coconut Macaroons

you could skip the dark chocolate . . . but why?   *Makes 6 dozen macaroons*

Macaroons have a whiff of old-fashioned elegance, like something out of a ladies' tearoom, that belies their simplicity. They're so easy, though—separating the eggs is about as complicated as it gets—that you'll have plenty of time to gussy them up with dark chocolate. You could use a 12-ounce bag of semisweet chips here, but I like to splurge on some good dark chocolate, such as Ghirardelli's 70% cacao. If you want to make a macaroon wreath as we've done here, add a good squeeze of green food coloring along with the vanilla and almond extracts.

> 6 egg whites
> 1¾ cups sugar
> 1 teaspoon salt
> 2 teaspoons vanilla extract
> ½ teaspoon pure almond extract
> 8 cups (about 21 ounces) flaked coconut
> 1½ cups heavy cream
> 12 ounces dark chocolate (such as Ghirardelli's 70% cacao bars)

1. Preheat the oven to 350°F and line 3 baking sheets with parchment paper.

2. In a large bowl, whisk the egg whites until frothy, then add the sugar, salt, vanilla, and almond extract, and whisk to dissolve the sugar. Stir in the coconut.

3. Drop the mixture by heaping tablespoons onto the prepared baking sheets, arranging them 4 across and 6 down, to fit 2 dozen onto each sheet. Bake them 18 to 20 minutes, until they are just turning golden around the edges. Cool the macaroons completely on the baking sheets.

4. While the macaroons cool, put the cream in a large, heavy saucepan over medium heat and heat just to boiling. Remove the pan from the heat and break the chocolate into pieces into the hot cream. Allow the mixture to sit for 3 minutes, then whisk until smooth.

5. Dip each macaroon into the chocolate to make a thick chocolate base. Lay the macaroon back on the parchment paper and proceed until all the cookies have been dipped. Place the baking sheets in the refrigerator for 30 minutes to firm up the chocolate. Store in airtight containers in the refrigerator for up to 2 weeks or in the freezer for up to 3 months. (In the freezer, the chocolate may develop white patches of "bloom," but it will fade as the macaroons rest at room temperature.)

No-Bake Chocolate-Oatmeal Clusters

sometimes there's no time to turn on the oven *Makes 6 dozen cookies*

I first made this cookie with my Girl Scout troop more decades ago than I care to discuss, and I remember being astonished that you could create cookies without baking! I made them for my family the very next day and for years after that. They are sort of candy-like in flavor, from the boiled sugar and butter, but they're decidedly cookie-shaped and oatmeal keeps them anchored in the cookie camp. Use old-fashioned rolled oats for the best flavor and chewiness. Quick oats don't have enough heft. It doesn't get much faster and easier to make a homemade treat, and these are still—thirty-some years after I first ate one—very, very tasty.

4 cups sugar

1 cup (2 sticks) butter

1 cup whole milk

½ cup unsweetened cocoa powder

1 cup creamy peanut butter

1 tablespoon vanilla extract

6 cups old-fashioned rolled oats

1. Line 3 baking sheets with wax or parchment paper. Put the sugar, butter, milk, and cocoa in a large, heavy-bottomed saucepan over medium-high heat and bring the mixture to a boil, stirring constantly. Continue to cook, stirring, for 1 minute, until the sugar is dissolved.

2. Blend in the peanut butter until fully combined, then stir in the vanilla. Add the oats, all at once, and stir to coat completely. A heatproof silicone spatula is very useful for scraping up the butter-sugar mixture from the edges and tossing it throughout the oats.

3. Drop the mixture by heaping tablespoons on the prepared baking sheets, making 6 rows of 4, or 24 cookies to a sheet. Cool them at room temperature until firm. You may need to place the baking sheets in the refrigerator for 10 to 15 minutes to firm up the cookies, but store them at room temperature in airtight containers for up to 1 week.

No-Bake Nutty Crunchies

The beauty of this no-bake recipe is its extreme versatility. You can use all sorts of variations for its different elements. For the peanut butter, it works just as well with chunky or creamy, regular or natural. For the "chip," use what you prefer from the endless range of what's available nowadays in the baking aisle, whether butterscotch or toffee or semisweet or milk or white chocolate. That said, I'd be a little dubious about using mint chips with peanut butter. You might also try a blend: half butterscotch and half white or darker chocolate, for example. And use something else crunchy if you like: instead of chow mein noodles, try Rice Krispies or cornflakes (or oatmeal, for a chewier cookie). And you can go nuts with the nuts: pecans, almonds, walnuts, cashews, peanuts, honey-roasted peanuts—it's your cookie, make what you like.

2 cups peanut butter

4 cups (24 ounces) butterscotch chips

2 cups chopped nuts

4 cups chow mein noodles

1 tablespoon vanilla extract

1. Line 3 baking sheets with wax or parchment paper.

2. Put the peanut butter and chips in a large, heavy-bottomed saucepan. Over medium-low heat, stir continually until the chips are melted and the mixture is smooth (unless you're using crunchy peanut butter, of course). Remove it from the heat and stir in the remaining ingredients. A heatproof silicone spatula is very useful for turning the mixture over to get it all combined.

3. Drop the mixture by heaping tablespoons onto the prepared baking sheets. They can be close together, so that you can fit 2 dozen onto each sheet. If the mixture starts to stiffen before you reach the end, rewarm it over low heat and stir for a few moments until it softens back up.

4. Let the cookies sit for an hour at room temperature until firm; if you have a warm kitchen, you may need to put them in the fridge for 20 minutes to help this process along. Store the cookies in airtight containers for up to 1 week (or 2 weeks in the refrigerator).

Sausage Balls page 103

CHAPTER FIVE

Here We Go A-Wassailing

Christmas Eve, Tree
Trimming, and
Carol Singing

I'm old enough now to know that the anticipation is everything. My children still believe that taking cookies off their countdown calendar (see page 53) and excitedly writing letters to Santa are just the lead-up to the main event, whereas I know that the lead-up *is* the main event. It's not that I don't enjoy Christmas Day, but certainly I'm not the first person to feel a strong sense of anticlimax. Perhaps Santa isn't bringing something fabulous enough for my stocking?

In any case, for me, the culmination of the holiday season is Christmas Eve. It's a much lower-key event than Christmas Day, with the unbearable excitement of gift opening and the inevitable let-down when it's all over. The night before, we enjoy the company of family and friends and eat ridiculously indulgent sweet and savory foods, wrap presents, and sing songs. How is that so different from the next day? Well, on Christmas Eve we have much more casual, indulgent foods, like sausage balls, cheese straws, and drinking custard (Southern staples from my Carolina childhood), as well as crazy-rich dips, such as Hot Spinach Dip, which includes both bacon and cream cheese. The British Isles' influence of my husband's Irish family has added dishes to our repertoire such as Sticky Toffee Pudding—really just an excuse to eat as much butter and sugar as any one person can possibly hold. Add we simply happen to love Queso Fundido, which might be best described, if you're not familiar with it, as a sort of Mexican cheese fondue.

Swedish meatballs are another holiday standard, since they were the stuff of Christmas Eve in my mother's youth, with her Swedish family that included grandparents who never learned English (and didn't even put their tree up until Christmas Eve—now, that's an approach to anticipation that my generation can hardly grasp!). We have so many favorites for Christmas Eve that over the years, some dishes inevitably appear earlier in the month, at tree trimmings, carol singings, and potlucks. It's only once—or twice, or three times—a year!

Caramelized Onion Dip

Makes about 3 cups dip

This recipe is my party trick, and I trot it out year-round. People who have only ever had store-bought onion dip or the kind made with a packet of soup mix actually moan when they taste it—it's that good. I like it best with potato chips, I confess, but it's so tasty that my kids will eat large quantities of raw vegetables when they can dip them into this. Don't rush the onions. They need time to caramelize to a deep, golden brown. Note that I dice them because they dip up better that way. Sliced onions leave you with strings of onion hanging down from your potato chip, which is less aesthetically pleasing.

I won't even add my secret ingredient to the list below, but here it is: 1 tablespoon fish sauce. You've either gotten onboard the fish-sauce bandwagon or you haven't, but if you have, you know it adds depth and richness—an indefinable feel of meatiness and body that's called umami. *This dip is delicious without fish sauce; with, sublime.*

- 2 tablespoons olive oil
- 2 large yellow onions, diced
- Salt to taste
- 1 cup mayonnaise
- 1 cup sour cream
- ¼ cup Worcestershire sauce
- 2 tablespoons Louisiana-style hot sauce (such as Crystal or Durkee's), or to taste
- ½ teaspoon freshly ground black pepper

1. Heat the olive oil in a large skillet over medium-low heat. Add the onions and a light sprinkling of salt. Cook slowly, stirring occasionally and reducing the heat if there's any hint of burning, until the onions are a deep, rich, golden brown, 30 to 40 minutes. Set them aside and let them cool to warm.

2. In a medium bowl, combine the remaining ingredients. Add the onions and stir well. Taste and adjust seasonings—I usually want a little more hot sauce, which adds not so much heat as brightness. You can eat the dip at once, or let it chill for several hours to meld the flavors.

Hot Spinach Dip

scoop it up hot with corn chips

I love cold spinach dip, the kind made from drained chopped frozen spinach and sour cream and mayonnaise. But that seems more like a warm-weather dish. Hot Spinach Dip is unabashedly hot and rich comfort food. The fact that it contains a package of frozen spinach can't possibly make up for all that bacon and cream cheese. It is excellent with corn chips, but it can also be served with crackers or those little squares of "party rye" or even with (gulp!) vegetables! You can present it in a pot over a warming candle, or you can spread it in an 8-inch square dish and bake it at 350°F for 15 minutes, until just bubbling. We like to leave it on the stove over very low heat and eat it right out of the pan.

6 slices bacon, diced

1 medium yellow onion, diced

2 garlic cloves, minced

1 package (10 ounces) frozen chopped spinach, thawed and drained

1 package (8 ounces) cream cheese

1 cup shredded Monterey Jack cheese

1 can (4 ounces) diced green chiles, drained

Corn chips or crackers, for dipping

1. In a skillet over medium heat, cook the bacon pieces until crisp. Remove them to a plate and set them aside.

2. Leave 2 tablespoons of bacon fat in the pan and remove the rest. Add the onion and garlic to the skillet and cook, stirring occasionally, until the onion is tender and golden, 6 to 7 minutes.

3. Add the spinach and stir to break it up and heat it through. Stir in the cream cheese and continue to cook for 3 to 4 minutes, until it is melted and creamy.

4. Add the Jack cheese, reserved bacon, and chiles and cook 2 or 3 minutes longer, until the cheese melts and the dip is well combined. Serve the dip warm.

Queso Fundido

Makes 4 to 6 servings

Ever share a plate of nachos with someone and find yourself chasing all the cheesy bits, trying to get your fair share before the other person eats all the cheese? Then you'll like Queso Fundido, since it's a whole dish of cheese, melted over chiles and chorizo and waiting to be scooped with tortilla chips or slathered on a warm soft tortilla. We think of it as a Christmas dish because at no other time of the year does it seem permissible to eat a pound of melted cheese. The moment it emerges from the oven is immensely festive! We use diced dry chorizo (the one that's more like pepperoni, not the fresh one that must be cooked), but if you can't find it, you can also use half a pound of spicy breakfast sausage, cooked until brown and well drained. Not authentic, but demonstrably delicious. I use poblanos for their mild, sweet heat, but any chile will do, and the same goes for the cheese. I like the creaminess of Monterey Jack combined with the tang of queso blanco, which crumbles when dry but melts into smoothness. You can combine cheeses; use whatever you like as long as it melts well and tastes good. This recipe doubles easily for a crowd, but if you double it, bake it in a 9-by-13-inch casserole.

> 2 tablespoons olive oil
> 1 large red onion, thinly sliced
> 2 garlic cloves, minced
> 2 to 3 poblano peppers, sliced, seeds discarded
> 4 ounces dry Spanish chorizo, diced small
> 8 ounces Monterey Jack cheese, grated
> 8 ounces queso blanco, crumbled
> Tortilla chips, for scooping

1. Preheat the oven to 400°F. Heat the oil in a large cast-iron skillet and cook the onion, garlic, and peppers until the onion is tender and slightly browned, 6 to 7 minutes.

2. Add the chorizo and cook to heat it through, another 2 to 3 minutes. Turn off the heat and spread the onions and peppers evenly across the bottom of the skillet. Sprinkle the Jack cheese evenly over the pan, then top it with the queso blanco.

3. Place the pan in the oven for 5 minutes, until the cheese is completely melted and barely starting to bubble. Serve at once, straight from the skillet, with tortilla chips. (Put an oven mitt over the skillet's handle so nobody forgets and grabs the hot handle in all the excitement.)

Sausage Balls

Early in my marriage, my husband, who's an excellent cook, saw me buying a box of Bisquick and a roll of spicy breakfast sausage, two foods that didn't generally grace our pantry, and his eyebrows shot into his hairline. This is one of those regional favorites that I grew up eating every Christmas without ever realizing that the rest of the world didn't eat them, too. Each holiday season, in home after home, any Southern hostess worth her salt trotted out a platter of sausage balls fresh from the oven. You didn't make them for family; they were the ultimate party food. The Internet is rife with variations on the recipe, but here's what I know about them: use the spiciest sausage and the extra-sharpest cheese you can find, and they shouldn't need added liquid. Bring the ingredients to room temperature, use your hands to combine everything, and—very important—serve hot.

> 1 pound hot, spicy breakfast sausage
> 2 cups (8 ounces) shredded extra-sharp cheddar (I use Cabot Hunter's cheddar)
> 2 cups Bisquick

1. Bring the sausage and cheese to room temperature and preheat the oven to 350°F.

2. Remove the casings from the sausages. Place the ingredients in a large bowl and mix with your hands until the mixture is completely combined, almost like a smooth paste. Roll it into 1-inch balls and place them on 2 rimmed baking sheets, leaving 1 inch between balls.

3. Bake for 20 to 25 minutes, until the sausage balls are puffed and golden brown. Serve them at once. (You can also freeze the baked sausage balls and reheat them for 10 minutes at 350°F.)

Mini Swedish Meatballs

Makes about 4 dozen meatballs

The Swedish-American Christmas celebrations of my mother's youth were extremely restrained affairs by today's standards. She grew up on a farm in far northern Minnesota, where the winters were long and cold, with short, dark days. By the time Christmas Eve rolled round, those hardy northern farmers enjoyed their day or two of frugal celebrations probably more than I could ever enjoy the festivities of the entire month. Swedish meatballs were a part of my mom's Christmas Eves past, and they're also part of mine. Keeping them small means they're easily picked up with toothpicks while grazing. A combination of pork, beef, and veal makes for better flavor and a lighter texture; you can often find all three packed together as "meatloaf mix."

2 slices white sandwich bread

¼ cup milk

1 egg

1 small yellow onion, minced

½ pound ground beef

½ pound ground veal

½ pound ground pork

1 teaspoon salt

¼ teaspoon freshly ground black pepper

¼ teaspoon freshly grated nutmeg

¼ teaspoon ground allspice

2 tablespoons butter

3 tablespoons all-purpose flour

3 cups beef broth (or chicken broth)

½ cup sour cream

1 tablespoon Dijon mustard

1. Tear the bread into pieces and put them into a large bowl; add the milk and egg. Stir to combine, then leave the mixture to soak for 5 minutes or so, until the bread soaks up the liquid.

2. Add the onion, meat, salt, pepper, nutmeg, and allspice, and mix well using your hands. Roll the mixture into 1-inch balls.

3. Heat the butter in a large skillet over medium-high heat, and begin frying the meatballs in batches, turning them so they brown on all sides, 6 to 8 minutes for each batch (lower the heat as needed to prevent burning). Set the cooked meatballs aside on a platter while you continue to cook.

4. When all the meatballs are done, leave 3 tablespoons of fat in the pan and discard the rest. Sprinkle the flour over the fat in the pan and stir, cooking for 1 to 2 minutes. Slowly pour in the broth, stirring constantly to prevent lumps. Cook for 5 or 6 minutes, until the sauce thickens. Stir in the sour cream and mustard, and cook for another minute or two to heat through.

5. Return all the meatballs to the pan and toss them in the sauce to heat them through. Serve hot.

Sticky Toffee Pudding

addictively sticky and sweet   *Makes 6 servings*

In the British Isles, this dessert is as ubiquitous on restaurant menus as cheesecake is over here. But Americans have been slow to warm up to Sticky Toffee Pudding, and I think it's merely that we've never had it, because this dessert has got it going on! It's not one of those curious, amusing British dishes with names like Spotted Dog or anything with treacle in it. Instead, it's a rich, super-moist cake that's drowned in a pool of warm caramel sauce—really, what's not to like? Don't let the dates put you off. They add moisture and a caramel undertone to the finished cake. It's overkill to pour a little heavy cream or dollop vanilla ice cream or whipped cream over the top, but don't let that stop you.

FOR THE PUDDING:

1½ cups chopped dates

1½ cups boiling water

1 teaspoon baking soda

½ cup (1 stick) butter, softened

½ cup sugar

2 eggs

1½ teaspoons vanilla extract

1¼ cups all-purpose flour

1½ teaspoons baking powder

FOR THE SAUCE:

1 cup heavy cream

1 cup dark brown sugar

½ cup (1 stick) butter

1 teaspoon vanilla extract

Whipped cream (optional)

1. Put the dates in a bowl and pour the boiling water over them. Stir in the baking soda and leave the mixture to soak until cool.

2. Preheat the oven to 350°F and butter a 2-quart baking dish. Cream the butter and granulated sugar with a mixer until fluffy, then beat in the eggs one at a time, mixing each one in well before adding the next.

3. Beat in the vanilla, then sift in half the flour and the baking powder and mix just until combined. Add the dates and their soaking water and mix, then add the remaining flour and mix just until combined. Smooth the batter into the prepared dish and bake until golden, 45 to 50 minutes.

4. While the cake bakes, put the cream, brown sugar, and butter in a heavy-bottomed saucepan over medium heat and bring it to a boil. Simmer until the sauce is slightly thickened, about 5 minutes. Remove the pan from the heat and stir in the vanilla.

5. Serve spoonfuls of the warm pudding with a generous helping of caramel sauce poured over each serving and a dollop of whipped cream.

Hot Chocolate Puddings

Makes 6 servings

These were inspired by a recipe of Nigella Lawson's that I first saw many years ago in her short-lived but brilliant column in the New York Times. I read it and thought, "Yep, that's for me," and I made it that same night and many, many other nights after. I have tinkered with it enough over the years to make it my own, including using a little less sugar. It's crucial to serve the puddings right out of the oven, so that the interiors are still just barely undercooked and hot when you add a dollop of whipped cream or ice cream. If you're serving them at the end of a meal, keep the oven hot while you eat and have the prepped puddings sitting on a baking sheet; pop them in the oven 10 minutes before you want dessert.

    You can vary the type of chips you add, whether white chocolate or butterscotch or mint or toffee—or leave them out altogether. When serving these to adults, I sometimes skip the extra chocolate and serve them instead with a cool and sharp raspberry sauce, made by blending a 10-ounce pack of frozen raspberries, slightly thawed, with 2 or 3 tablespoons confectioners' sugar and 1 tablespoon lemon juice.

½ cup (1 stick) butter, plus more for greasing the ramekins

4 ounces bittersweet chocolate (such as Ghirardelli's 60% cacao bar)

½ cup sugar

¼ teaspoon salt

3 eggs

1½ teaspoons vanilla extract (or ½ teaspoon pure almond extract)

3 tablespoons flour

½ cup semisweet chocolate chips

Whipped cream or vanilla ice cream, to serve

1. Preheat the oven to 400°F and generously butter six 6-ounce ramekins. Set the ramekins on a baking sheet.

2. Put the butter in a medium-size, microwavable mixing bowl and break up the chocolate bar into it. Microwave on high for 1 minute, then stir. Microwave in additional 10-second blasts if needed, stirring in between, to just melt the chocolate. Stir until smooth.

3. Add the sugar and salt and stir to combine. Break in the eggs and beat them in vigorously. Stir in the vanilla, then add the flour and chocolate chips and stir just to combine.

4. Divide the mixture among the ramekins and bake it for 8 to 10 minutes, just until the tops look set and a little cracked, and the interiors are still a bit liquid. Serve the puddings hot, with a dollop of whipped cream or ice cream on top to melt down into the hot chocolate interior when you break the surface with your spoon.

Panettone Bread Pudding

I don't mean to suggest that I'm not a fan of panettone, but I often recommend doing things with it other than simply eating it (see also the Panettone French Toast on page 120). So much packaged panettone is a bit stale and dull by the time you open it, and you can restore some of the glory by elevating it to a new dish. Panettone bread pudding is a perfect holiday dessert, since it's simple to make and deeply tasty, with the satisfying crunch of the toasted bread edges playing off the creamy custard. Lightly buttering each slice keeps the panettone from dissolving into mush in the cream and adds lushness to the pudding. The dish has two other advantages: you can use up an entire 1-pound loaf and kids love it. I don't like the custard excessively sweet since the bread is already sweetened, so I add sugar with a restrained hand, but you could easily add an additional ¼ cup, even ½ cup more. If you aren't cooking for kids, try putting a couple tablespoons of Grand Marnier in the egg mixture.

¼ cup (½ stick) butter, softened, plus more for greasing

1 loaf (1 pound) panettone, quartered and then cut into slices ¾ inch thick

6 eggs

3 cups milk

1 cup heavy cream

½ cup sugar

1 tablespoon vanilla extract

Grated zest of 1 orange

Whipped cream, for serving (optional)

1. Preheat the oven to 350°F and butter a 9-by-13-inch baking dish. Lightly butter the slices of panettone and lay them, slightly overlapping, in the baking dish.

2. Whisk the eggs in a large bowl, then add the remaining ingredients. Pour the mixture evenly over the bread in the dish and let it rest for 10 minutes, pressing the bread down gently a few times and allowing the bread to soak up the egg mixture.

3. Bake the pudding for 40 to 45 minutes, until it's puffed and golden. Serve warm, in slices. (My husband swears that warm bread pudding must have a dollop of cool whipped cream on top, which is clearly madness, but so good.)

Drinking Custard

Makes about 1½ quarts, 8 to 10 servings

My elderly great-aunt in West Tennessee made the best "drinking custard" I have ever tasted. Also known as "boiled custard," it's not very sweet or thick; it was a thin custard served in small glasses and drunk with great gusto at holiday parties, where a huge kettle of it would be kept warm on the front of the stove. I remember getting a glassful right before bed, when we children were already in our pajamas, and it was such an exciting special treat that our little hands practically trembled as we clutched the glasses. My great-aunt cooked and stirred her custard until it coated the back of a sterling silver spoon and ran off in a sheet, rather than running off in streams, and that's still the best measure of its doneness that I've found. Taste while it's cooking and add a little more sugar if it's not sweet enough for you. Boiled custard can be served warm or cold; I like it both ways. When we were kids, our mom always let us stir a little extra vanilla into each serving.

> 1½ quarts (6 cups) whole milk
> 8 egg yolks
> ¾ cup sugar
> ½ teaspoon salt
> 1 tablespoon vanilla extract

1. Put the milk in a large pot over medium heat and begin to heat it, stirring occasionally, until a few bubbles appear around the edges (don't let it boil). Set a large saucepan of water to heat to a simmer.

2. While the milk heats, whisk together the egg yolks, sugar, and salt in a large, heatproof bowl. Ladle a cupful of the hot milk into the bowl, whisking continuously, then slowly ladle in the rest, continuing to whisk. Set the bowl on top of the large saucepan of simmering water.

3. Cook, stirring constantly, until the custard starts to thicken, 6 to 8 minutes. It should remain at a low simmer, with only a few bubbles rising. When the mixture starts to thicken (or when it coats the back of a metal spoon—it needn't be silver!), remove the pot from the heat and stir in the vanilla. Serve the custard warm, at room temperature, or chilled.

Rich and Creamy Eggnog

The standard warning about not using raw eggs when cooking for children, the elderly, or those with compromised immune systems is no joke. When I make this eggnog for guests, I am fortunate enough to be able to use eggs bought directly from a farmer we know, so I feel confident in serving it to family. I also know that everyone is not so lucky, so I highly recommend pasteurizing your store-bought eggs by the method I suggest below. You can also buy liquid pasteurized egg in some supermarkets, but then you can't separate the eggs and whip the whites. Homemade eggnog, without liquor, was a standard of my childhood, and as an adult I've found I like it even more with a little brandy and rum in it! Add that to individual adult cups, and leave the balance unadulterated for younger taste buds.

12 eggs

4 cups heavy cream

1½ cups sugar

6 cups milk

2 tablespoons vanilla extract

Grated zest of 1 orange

½ teaspoon freshly grated nutmeg, plus additional for sprinkling

1. Pasterize your eggs if needed: Put the whole eggs in a large saucepan and cover them with water. Place the pan over high heat and heat to 140°F. Use an instant-read thermometer and do not walk away from the pan. Turn off the heat as soon as you hit 140 and let the eggs sit for 3 to 4 minutes. Immediately pour off the hot water and cover them with cool water. The eggs should still be liquid inside. Separate the yolks and whites into 2 large bowls.

2. Using an electric mixer, beat the whites until soft peaks form and set them aside. Put 2 cups of the heavy cream in a bowl and beat the cream until stiff, then set the whipped cream aside.

3. Using the same beaters, in another bowl (no shortcuts here, sadly!), beat the yolks with the sugar until they turn pale and thick. With the mixer on the lowest speed, blend in the milk, the remaining 2 cups cream, vanilla, orange zest, and nutmeg.

4. Fold in the egg whites and the whipped cream. Spoon the eggnog into cups and grate more fresh nutmeg over the top. Serve immediately.

Sparkling Cranberry Punch

festive Christmas quaff

Makes 2 quarts, about 8 servings

"Punch" sounds so quaint and old-fashioned these days, but I remember it fondly from the ladies' teas, showers, and wedding receptions of my youth. I can't think when I last saw a big crystal bowl of punch at an event, but when I made a bowlful of this red holiday beverage for a recent children's gathering, they fell upon it like dehydrated little monkeys and demanded more. It was bubbly and festive, a good way to avoid serving soda, and a nice change from juice boxes. You can add the frozen strawberries or raspberries as you like. In my house, one son loves the floating, thawing berries, and the other hates them (hmm, like pretty much everything else). I like this punch with seltzer, since all the juices are already pretty sweet, but kids seem to like it best with ginger ale. I remember a friend of my mother's who made a similar punch and, just before serving, turned a quart of raspberry sherbet into the bowl, where it fizzed and melted. Messy but delicious.

    4 cups cranberry juice cocktail, chilled
    1 can (6 ounces) frozen limeade concentrate
    1 cup orange juice, chilled
    4 cups seltzer or ginger ale, chilled
    1 package (10 ounces) frozen strawberries or raspberries (optional)
    1 lime, thinly sliced

1. In a large jug or a punch bowl, combine the cranberry juice, frozen limeade, and orange juice.

2. Just before serving, add the seltzer or ginger ale, then float the berries and lime slices on top. Serve at once.

Christmas Frittata page 118

Frosted Cinnamon Buns page 128

CHAPTER SIX

Christmas
Morning

❋

Goodies to Go with
Gift Opening

When I was growing up, a hefty Christmas breakfast was a must before opening presents. It stretched out the sweet anticipation and made the day last longer. As children, we couldn't imagine why we had to wait so long, and we all knew families where the kids were allowed to fall on their gifts and open them instantly, but my parents liked to draw out the process, and as we got older, we came to appreciate it. One of our favorite Christmas breakfasts was waffles with whipped orange-honey butter, and making enough waffles for a family of six took enough time that the anticipation was very drawn out indeed! The waffles were usually accompanied by eggs and bacon, so we were prepared for tearing paper off packages, and also full enough to make it through to the other main meal of the day, Christmas dinner, which might be many, many hours after that enormous breakfast.

With my own children, I keep up the tradition of eating before presents, and I like to think that it's a valuable learning experience to have gratification delayed. It's hard to pretend that we're delaying any kind of pleasure, however, when the holiday breakfast is something like crumb-topped coffee cake, or freshly fried doughnuts dipped in warm maple syrup, or cinnamon rolls fragrant and tender under a swirl of cream cheese frosting.

The beauty of most of these is that you can prep them the night before or, as with the super-fluffy pancakes or the Christmas version of French toast—which puts to ideal use one of those ubiquitous boxes of panettone—throw them together fast in the morning. Lay down a savory base with an eggy casserole or a cheesy frittata dotted with holiday colors of red and green. Either way, you'll be extremely well fortified for the day's exertions.

Christmas Morning Casserole

Makes 6 to 8 servings

Breakfast casseroles are also called strata, *from the Italian for "layers," but they are not really layered; they're a mix of cheese, meat, egg, and bread that soaks overnight and bakes up like a soufflé. Some recipes call for sweet or hot Italian sausage, but I like to use a roll of sage-scented breakfast sausage, such as Jimmy Dean. That tastes more like morning to me, and less like the spicy base of something for dinner. That said, you can vary the ingredients to suit your taste, with a different cheese or sausage or diced ham, and with or without the Christmassy addition of diced red pepper and chopped green onion (my kids don't love that, but hey, the colors look great!). The only important thing is to use soft white bread from the supermarket and not a chewy baguette nor sliced bread from a plastic bag. You want the big loaves marked French or Italian, cut into large cubes, so they can soak up the egg and milk overnight, disintegrate into the casserole, and puff up when the dish hits the hot oven.*

- 1 pound breakfast sausage, mild or spicy
- 1 pound French or Italian bread, cut into 1-inch cubes (about 8 cups)
- 8 ounces extra-sharp cheddar cheese (about 2 cups grated)
- 3 scallions, white and green parts thinly sliced
- 1 small red bell pepper, diced small
- 8 eggs
- 2 cups whole milk
- ½ teaspoon freshly ground black pepper

1. Remove the casings from the sausage and cook it in a skillet over medium heat until it is lightly browned, breaking it up into pieces as it fries, 8 to 10 minutes.

2. While the sausage cooks, lightly grease a glass 9-by-13-inch baking dish, fill it with the bread cubes, and scatter the cheese, scallions, and bell pepper over the bread. Use a slotted spoon to lift the cooked sausage into the glass dish and spread it over the top, leaving the fat in the skillet.

3. In a large bowl, whisk the eggs. Stir in the milk and black pepper. Pour the mixture evenly over the casserole, then cover the dish with plastic wrap and refrigerate it overnight.

4. When you are ready to proceed, preheat the oven to 350°F, remove the plastic wrap, and bake the casserole for 45 to 55 minutes, until it's puffed and golden brown. Serve warm.

Christmas Frittata

it's a little bit cheesy

Sometimes it's a toss-up for me whether I've made an omelet or a frittata. I might have intended to make an omelet, but I've so laden it with ingredients that it won't flip over, and instead I put a proud heap of egg and filling on a platter and proudly declare it "frittata!" But a real frittata is more of an egg cake, with tasty ingredients neatly suspended in it. It has the added virtue, unlike an omelet, of being good at room temperature, even cool. The only extra trouble is that to cook the egg all the way through, you usually end up having to run it under the broiler. Using a really creamy cheese like Havarti makes this one taste extra-festive, but cheddar or anything else you like works beautifully here. The Parmesan is not strictly necessary, but it adds saltiness and an extra layer of flavor.

4 slices bacon, diced

1 yellow onion, minced

6 eggs

¼ cup whole milk

1½ cups grated soft cheese, such as Havarti

¼ cup grated Parmesan

2 scallions, white and green parts thinly sliced

½ teaspoon freshly grated black pepper

3 cooked red potatoes, skin on, diced

2 cups fresh baby spinach leaves

1. Preheat the broiler on high. Put the bacon pieces in a large, heatproof skillet and turn on the heat to medium. Cook until the bacon browns and renders its fat, then add the onion and cook, stirring occasionally, until the pieces are tender and translucent, 6 to 7 minutes.

2. While the onion cooks, whisk the eggs and milk in a medium bowl. Stir in the Havarti, Parmesan, scallions, and pepper. Set the mixture aside.

3. Put the potatoes and spinach leaves in the skillet and cook just to heat the potatoes through and wilt the spinach, 2 to 3 minutes. Shake the skillet to evenly distribute the ingredients, and then stir up the egg and cheese mixture again and pour it carefully over all.

4. Cook the frittata for about 4 minutes, until the bottom of the egg is set, then put the pan under the broiler for 2 or 3 minutes, until the surface is puffed and golden. Don't leave it; watch carefully, because it can go from beautiful to ruined in no time!

5. Turn the frittata out onto a serving platter (if you're worried you'll damage it during the flip, you can also use 2 spatulas to lift it carefully onto the platter faceup). Serve it hot or at room temperature. It's even good cold out of the fridge the next day.

Perfect Christmas Pancakes

a recipe to use all year long   *Makes 6 large pancakes*

Even flat, thin pancakes are excellent with plenty of maple syrup, but if you've ever been disappointed that your pancakes don't get fluffy and high, this recipe is for you. It's got baking powder and baking soda and buttermilk. In the baking world, this is like wearing suspenders with a belt. I like to scoff at that kind of doubling up myself, since it suggests that—ha!—the recipe writer doesn't understand the most basic tenets of quick-rise chemistry. But have faith and go with it: the thick batter makes for pancakes that are mile-high and, thanks to all that buttermilk and butter (sigh), they taste amazing. Keep the last 2 tablespoons of butter from the stick to grease the pan occasionally while cooking, since it helps the pancakes cook up beautifully with the faintest crispy edge.

One more crucial detail: do not overmix! You know how all pancake recipes say things like "stir just to combine" or "until a few lumps remain"? Really, just barely stir the wet ingredients into the dry. Let clumps remain, with actual hints of white flour still visible in the batter. You'll be rewarded with pancakes that look like a magazine photo shoot.

2¼ cups all-purpose flour (or 1¼ cups all-purpose flour and 1 cup whole-wheat flour)

2 tablespoons sugar

1½ teaspoons baking powder

1 teaspoon baking soda

6 tablespoons butter, plus additional for greasing the pan

1½ cups buttermilk

2 eggs

1. In a large bowl, whisk together the flour, sugar, baking powder, and baking soda. In a microwavable bowl, melt the butter in the microwave (1 minute on high will probably do it), then whisk in the buttermilk and eggs.

2. Preheat a griddle or large frying pan over medium-high heat, using a little butter (or some vegetable oil, if you prefer) to grease the pan. When water droplets bounce on the hot surface (I run a couple fingers under the tap and shake my hand over the pan to release a few drops), pour the wet ingredients into the dry and stir as briefly as possible to barely combine.

3. Ladle the batter into the hot pan by the ½ cup. Cook on the first side for 2 to 3 minutes, until each pancake looks dry around the edges and the center just starts to bubble. Flip and cook on the second side for 1 to 2 minutes, until just cooked through.

4. Repeat with the remaining batter, adjusting the heat as necessary to keep the pancakes from browning too quickly. If you're not serving as you cook (we're savages at my house and we cook and eat, cook and eat!), keep the pancakes warm on a platter in a 185° F oven.

Sour Cream Waffles

slathered with fluffy honey-orange butter

*Makes about 6 servings
(12 waffles or so, depending on your waffle-maker)*

Sour cream not only makes these waffles taste rich and hearty, but it also gives them an extremely toothsome texture. There's just enough sugar in the batter that the outside becomes crisp in the waffle iron while the inside stays tender. If you don't like the idea of hovering over the waffle iron on Christmas morning (though waffle-making does have a certain festive air about it), you can make these up to a week before and freeze them. When you're ready to eat, put the frozen waffles on a baking sheet and heat them at 350°F for 10 to 12 minutes, until they're hot and crisp. Store any leftovers in the freezer, and you can drop them in the toaster for solitary breakfasts.

FOR THE HONEY-ORANGE BUTTER:

1/2 cup (1 stick) butter, softened

1/4 cup honey

2 tablespoons juice and zest of 1 orange

FOR THE WAFFLES:

2 eggs, separated

1 1/2 cups sour cream

6 tablespoons butter, melted

1½ teaspoons vanilla extract

2½ cups all-purpose flour

3 tablespoons sugar

1 teaspoon baking soda

1. Using a stand or hand mixer, whip the softened butter with the honey, orange juice, and zest in a large bowl for 2 to 3 minutes, until light and fluffy. Set aside at room temperature.

2. In a spotlessly clean bowl (no hint of grease!), beat the egg whites until they are stiff but not dry.

3. In a large bowl, whisk together the egg yolks with the sour cream, melted butter, and vanilla. Sift the flour, sugar, and baking soda directly over the wet ingredients and stir just to combine (don't stir till it's smooth, or you'll beat out all the air bubbles from the baking soda combining with the sour cream, and your waffles won't have as much lift).

4. Gently fold the beaten egg whites into the batter and cook according to the manufacturer's instructions for your waffle iron. If you're cooking all the waffles at once before eating them (rather than having your family waiting to fork up the next one as soon as the waffle iron opens), set the finished waffles on a heatproof platter in a 185°F oven until ready to serve.

Hot Maple Doughnuts

have plenty of napkins at hand   *Makes 24 small doughnuts*

These plumptious little bundles of warm dough may be the best doughnuts you'll ever eat. Don't be tempted to add more flour, even though the dough seems very soft. All will come out right when they hit the hot oil. Frying is surprisingly quick and easy, and they're perfect simply rolled in the spicy sugar. Once you add that dish of warm maple syrup for dipping (I prefer Grade B, which is darker and more potent than Grade A), you have a breakfast treat that threatens to take the focus off opening gifts!

2 tablespoons butter

¾ cup milk

3 tablespoons granulated sugar

1 package active dry yeast (2¼ teaspoons)

1 teaspoon vanilla extract

2 cups all-purpose flour

1 teaspoon salt

3 egg yolks

Vegetable oil for frying

¾ cup light brown sugar

2 teaspoons ground cinnamon

½ teaspoon freshly grated nutmeg

1 cup real maple syrup

1. Melt the butter in the milk in a microwavable bowl by nuking them for 1 to 2 minutes on high. Afterward, use an instant-read thermometer to make sure the milk is no hotter than 115°F. If it is, cool it for a few minutes. Stir in the 3 tablespoons sugar and add the yeast. Let the mixture sit for 10 minutes until the surface is foamy.

2. In the bowl of a stand mixer, combine the milk mixture and the vanilla. Add the flour and salt, mixing well. Add the egg yolks, one at a time, mixing well after each. Cover the bowl with plastic wrap and let the dough rise at room temperature for 40 minutes (or overnight in the refrigerator).

3. Turn the dough out onto a floured surface and divide it into 24 pieces, rolling each one into a ball with your palms. Arrange the balls on a greased baking sheet, cover them lightly with plastic wrap, and let them rise in a warm place for 20 minutes.

4. Put 2 inches of oil in the bottom of a large, heavy saucepan and heat it over medium-high heat to 350°F on a frying thermometer. Fry the doughnuts in batches, turning them now and then,

continued

until each one is a rich golden brown, about 4 minutes for each batch. (Try to keep the oil's heat constant for best results.) Drain the doughnuts on a platter lined with paper towels and keep them warm while you finish cooking the remaining doughnuts.

5. Mix the brown sugar, cinnamon, and nutmeg in a medium bowl and toss the doughnuts in it, in batches. Put the maple syrup in a microwavable bowl and heat it in the microwave for 1 minute on high, just until warmed. Serve the sugared doughnuts at once with the maple syrup for dipping.

Panettone French Toast

what to do with the second half of the loaf

Makes 6 to 8 servings

Panettone, the Italian enriched sweet bread studded with bits of orange and dried fruit, was once a rare treat. Then those colorful, squared-off boxes began to proliferate. Suddenly, you'd be wandering through your local drugstore in July and would stumble across a mountain of them with a big "Sale!" sign on top. Unless you've got a particularly exquisite loaf from a well-known bakery or, say, a friend's kitchen, then making French toast, or the Panettone Bread Pudding on page 109, is the best thing to do with the deluge of (sort of dry) panettone that hits American shores around the holidays. Some panettone is sweeter than others, some has more fruit and spice. If you have a blander panettone, you may want to add a little sugar and cinnamon to the egg and milk mixture. Either way, adding orange zest highlights the orangey flavor that should be in all panettone.

I pound panettone

6 eggs

2 cups whole milk

Grated zest of I orange

I teaspoon vanilla extract

2 tablespoons sugar (optional)

I teaspoon ground cinnamon (optional)

Butter for cooking

Confectioners' sugar

Maple syrup

1. Preheat the oven to 185°F. Slice the panettone thickly, ¾ to 1 inch. In a large, shallow bowl, whisk the eggs with the milk, then whisk in the orange zest and vanilla, along with the sugar and cinnamon, if using.

2. Preheat a large skillet or griddle over medium-high heat and lightly grease it with butter. Dip the slices of bread in the egg and milk mixture, flipping them to soak them completely. Lay them in the hot pan and cook, 2 to 3 minutes per side, until they're golden brown. Transfer the cooked slices to a platter in the oven as you finish cooking the rest.

3. Repeat with remaining panettone slices. Sift a little confectioners' sugar over the platter and serve with maple syrup.

Christmas Morning Bubble Bread

You might know it as monkey bread, but we knew it as "bubble bread" when I was growing up, thanks to the round balls of dough that kept their shape because they'd been dipped in butter, sugar, and spices before going into the pan. Adding a hint of ground cardamom and some vanilla to the buttery sugar makes these better than the ordinary, so they're ideal fare for Christmas morning. Dipping the dough is a little untidy, but kids will be delighted to assist you in that task, so put them at the kitchen table with their butter and dough, and just plan to sponge up the mess when they're done. It will keep them busy while you wrap a few last gifts. Then put the Bundt pan full of dough balls in the refrigerator to rise overnight, so you can bake it in the morning with no hassle.

4 tablespoons granulated sugar

1 package active dry yeast (2¼ teaspoons)

¾ cup warm milk (about 115°F)

1 teaspoon salt

2 eggs

¾ cup (1½ sticks) butter, softened

2¾ to 3 cups all-purpose flour

¾ cup light brown sugar

1 teaspoon vanilla extract

1 teaspoon ground cinnamon

½ teaspoon ground cardamom

¼ teaspoon freshly grated nutmeg

1. Whisk 2 tablespoons of the sugar and the yeast into the warm milk and let it sit for 10 minutes, until there's a frothy head on top.

2. In a large bowl, combine the milk and yeast mixture with the remaining 2 tablespoons sugar, the salt, eggs, and 4 tablespoons of the butter and whisk to combine. (The butter may not be fully incorporated yet.) Gradually stir in the flour to make a soft dough.

3. Put the dough in a greased bowl, cover it with plastic wrap, and let it rise in a warm place for 2 hours.

4. Melt the remaining stick of butter and put it in a small bowl. In another small bowl, combine the brown sugar, vanilla, and spices. Turn the dough out onto a lightly floured surface and use a sharp knife to divide it into 24 pieces. The dough will be very soft, but don't be tempted to add flour. Dip each piece into the melted butter, then turn it in the spiced sugar to coat and place it in a 12-cup Bundt or tube pan.

5. When all the pieces of dough are stacked evenly in the pan, pour any remaining sugar and butter over the bread. Cover the pan loosely with plastic wrap and let the dough ring rise in a warm place for 1 hour or place it in the refrigerator to rise slowly overnight.

6. When you are ready to bake, preheat the oven to 400°F. Bake the bread for 10 minutes, then lower the heat to 350°F and bake for an additional 10 to 15 minutes, until the bubble bread is puffy and golden. Instantly invert it onto a serving platter, letting any additional sugar syrup in the pan drip over the top. Serve at once.

Frosted Cinnamon Buns

hard to say no to cream cheese frosting *Makes 18 rolls*

The fact that these buns contain so much butter explains both why they're so exquisitely tender and good, and also why they're a treat to reserve for Christmas morning. The eggy, buttery dough is so rich that it's nearly like brioche. A hint of orange with the cream cheese keeps the sweet frosting from being cloying. You can make the rolls the evening before and let them rise overnight in the refrigerator. In the morning, just pop them in the oven, then frost them while they're still warm.

FOR THE BUNS:

1¼ cups milk

½ cup (1 stick) butter, softened

1 package active dry yeast (2¼ teaspoons)

½ cup light brown sugar

1 egg

1 teaspoon ground cinnamon

½ teaspoon salt

4½ cups all-purpose flour, plus more as needed

FOR THE FILLING:

½ cup (1 stick) butter, softened

1 cup dark brown sugar

1 cup chopped pecans

1 tablespoon ground cinnamon

FOR THE FROSTING:

½ cup (1 stick) butter, softened

4 ounces cream cheese, softened

2 cups confectioners' sugar

2 tablespoons orange juice

1 teaspoon vanilla extract

1. To make the dough, in a small saucepan, heat the milk and butter just until the butter is melted. Remove the pan from the heat and cool the mixture to 115°F. (If the mixture is any hotter, it may kill your yeast.) Add the yeast and brown sugar to the pan and stir to combine. Let sit for 10 minutes, until the mixture is frothy.

2. Put the milk mixture into a stand mixer fitted with a dough hook and beat in the egg, cinnamon, and salt. Add the flour, 1 cup at a time, mixing until one addition is combined before adding more. (If the dough seems firm enough, you may not need the final ½ cup.) Knead the mixture using the dough hook for 4 to 5 minutes, until the dough is springy and elastic.

3. Turn the dough out of the bowl and lightly coat the inside of the bowl with vegetable oil (it's not necessary to clean the bowl first). Put the dough back in the bowl, turning to coat it a little in the oil, then cover it with plastic wrap and let it rise in a warm place about 2 hours, until doubled.

4. Use 1 tablespoon of the softened butter for the filling to grease the bottom of a 9-by-13-inch glass baking dish. Turn the dough out onto a lightly floured work surface. Roll it out into a large rectangle, about 8 inches by 12 inches. Spread the dough with the remaining softened butter, then sprinkle it with the brown sugar, being sure not to miss the edges. Sprinkle with the pecans and cinnamon, then roll up the dough from one of the long sides, pinching the seam to seal it.

5. Use a serrated knife to cut 18 rolls, then arrange them in the baking dish, cover it with plastic wrap, and let the rolls rise in the refrigerator overnight, or for about 1 hour at room temperature.

6. When you're ready to bake, preheat the oven to 375°F. Bake the rolls for 18 to 20 minutes, until they are well risen and the tops are turning gold. Be careful not to overbake them, or they'll dry out. Turn them out onto a cooling rack, letting any extra sugar or butter drip over the tops.

7. While the rolls are cooling slightly, use a mixer to combine the frosting ingredients. Flip the rolls over and frost them while they're still warm. Serve at once.

Streusel-Topped Marble Coffee Cake

buttery topping on meltingly tender cake

Makes 8 to 10 servings

I love moist, fresh coffee cake, and nothing is more disappointing than a dry, dull one without enough topping or filling. This version hits all the high notes: a moist, rich sour cream cake that's not terribly sweet, marbled with brown sugar and cinnamon, and topped with a thick layer of buttery, sugary streusel. You could bake this the day before you plan to serve it, and the cake will still be wonderfully moist, but the streusel won't be so crisp and melting as it is right out of the oven. One option is to prep the cake batter and then let it sit overnight, crumbs and all, under plastic wrap in the refrigerator. In the morning, put the cake pan in the cold oven while you heat it up to 350°F, then bake it for the usual time once the oven hits its temperature. It won't rise quite as high, but it will still be delicious—and freshly baked.

FOR THE STREUSEL:
½ cup (1 stick) butter, melted
½ cup granulated sugar
½ cup light brown sugar
1 teaspoon ground cinnamon
1½ cups all-purpose flour
½ teaspoon salt
1½ cups all-purpose flour
1½ cups pecan halves

FOR THE CAKE:
½ cup (1 stick) butter, softened
½ cup sugar
1 cup sour cream
2 eggs
1½ teaspoons vanilla extract
2 cups all-purpose flour
1 teaspoon baking soda

FOR THE MARBLING:
½ cup light brown sugar
2 teaspoons ground cinnamon

continued

1. Preheat the oven to 350°F and generously butter a 9-by-13-inch pan.

2. Mix the streusel ingredients except for the pecans in a medium bowl, using your hands to press everything together. It will be stiff and thick.

3. To make the cake, put the butter and sugar in a bowl and use a mixer to cream until fluffy. Beat in the sour cream, followed by the eggs, one at a time. Mix in the vanilla, then add the flour and baking soda, mixing just until smooth.

4. Spoon the batter into the prepared pan. In a small bowl or cup, combine the brown sugar and cinnamon for the filling. Spoon this over the cake batter. Take the tip of a knife and drag it over the cake, turning and twisting to streak and marble the cinnamon sugar throughout the batter.

5. Use your hands to pick up big clumps of the streusel and drop them all over the surface of the cake. Scatter the pecan halves over the top. Bake for 20 to 25 minutes, until the cake is golden brown on top and a tester inserted in the center comes out with a few crumbs clinging to it. Serve warm.

Spiced Christmas Coffee

My mother's side of the family hails from northern Minnesota, only a couple generations out of Sweden. So my summer vacations as a kid were spent among people with a fondness for pastry and cardamom and coffee, lots of coffee. Anyone who's ever spent time among either real Swedes or the Scandinavians of Minnesota knows that both cultures, as far apart as they now are, produce prodigious coffee drinkers. My dear grandmother's coffeepot worked hard all day, each and every day, from the first cup in the morning to the final little pot she brewed at night to help her to relax before bed.

As a kid, I didn't know that what the relatives called "Swedish egg coffee," with an egg broken into the grounds to smooth and clarify, was a beverage unknown in the mother country, but to me it brings back a kitchen tableful of women from many generations, laughing and talking. I don't drink eighteen cups of coffee a day myself, so I don't bother boiling water and coffee grounds and breaking in an entire egg, which settles when a cup of cold water is poured in. Instead, throughout the holidays, I employ my grandmother's shortcut for her drip coffee-maker: broken eggshell with the hints of white still clinging to it, in the filter, along with a few spices. The result is coffee that's clear and smooth, less acid, with a faint hint of spice that's much more subtle (and delicious) than the excesses of coffee with artificial flavorings.

½ cup ground coffee

Shell (both halves) from 1 freshly broken egg

2 whole cardamom pods, slightly crushed

½ cinnamon stick

3 to 4 whole cloves

1. Fill the reservoir of your automatic drip coffee-maker with water to make 8 cups of coffee.

2. Put the coffee in the filter, then add the still-damp eggshell. Sprinkle the coffee with the cardamom, cinnamon, and cloves.

3. Brew as usual. Milk and a hint of sugar bring out the subtle flavor of the lightly spiced coffee.

Irish Plum Pudding page 137

CHAPTER SEVEN

Making Merry

✳

Festivities and Traditions
from Other Countries
and Cultures

This whirlwind tour of terrific holiday treats from all around the world is by no means exhaustive. Instead, it represents the goodies that have found their way into our home via the traditions of our own blended families, travel, and the generosity of friends. The "Swedishness" of my mother's side of the family was most apt to emerge at Christmastime, and we never skipped the rice pudding for Christmas Eve dinner. Most years we also managed to make buns for Saint Lucia Day, whether or not we managed to make them on the actual day, December 13. The buns were oddly reminiscent in flavor of another tradition from my childhood holidays, a "lovefeast" at a Moravian church in Winston-Salem, North Carolina. There, strangers from all walks of life gathered to join in song in a church fragrant with the scent of beeswax candles and the smell of the milky sweet coffee served with large, mildly sweet buns so that everyone could break bread together.

Thanks to those industrious Moravian settlers who came to the area in the seventeenth century seeking religious freedom, anyone who grew up near Old Salem, as the restored village is called, tends to be obsessed with Moravian sugar cake, a flat, yeast-raised, potato-enriched dough that's dotted with butter and sugar. Since I can't always get it wherever I am, I've had to learn to make it myself, and it's well worth the effort, as are all the goodies in this chapter, from the sweetly sticky delights of *turrones*, a nutty nougat from the Cuban holiday table, to the elaborate mysteries of the plum pudding and Christmas cake without which my Irish husband's holidays would be sad indeed!

Irish Plum Pudding

Having married into an Irish family some twenty years ago, I now have a long history with Christmas plum pudding, but when I first tasted it, it was a source of awe and mystery. Plum pudding figures largely in British literature, not least in A Christmas Carol, *but many, many Americans have never tasted it. And that's a shame, because there's nothing else like it on the American dessert table. If chocolate chip cookies are soda pop, plum pudding is a vintage wine, long-aged, with depths and flavors that are more than the sum of its parts. It was traditionally made with suet, but in Ireland of recent years, puddings made with butter have predominated, and although they come out darker, they taste a little lighter.*

For American tastes, the milder flavor of a butter-based pudding can be a good thing because, I confess, at first glance, plum pudding looks pretty unprepossessing on the plate. Before you set it alight, it's merely a large half-round, dark brown and glistening. The Irish get around this by setting it spectacularly aflame, bringing it to the table with a plume of burning brandy wreathing it like a small, smoldering volcano. Once extinguished, it's sliced into wedges with great fanfare and in some houses eaten with a topping of brandy butter, which is sort of like a light caramel sauce. We usually eat ours with whipped cream that has been enhanced with brown sugar and a dollop of brandy—yes, even the kids eat this, so lightly do we lace our home version.

If you're a lover of Dickens and you've never had plum pudding before, you owe it to yourself to try it at least once. And don't forget, while you're stirring it all together, to invite everyone present in the house to come into the kitchen for a stir. It's supposed to bring good luck for all the coming year.

At my in-laws' home, it's their tradition to fry a few slices of leftover plum pudding in butter to accompany the eggs and bacon at the next morning's breakfast.

1 cup light brown sugar

Grated zest and juice of 1 orange

Grated zest and juice of 1 lemon

1 cup dried currants

1 cup golden raisins

1 cup dark raisins

½ cup candied cherries

½ cup candied orange peel (see Pamelas, page 35 to make your own)

1 bottle (12 ounces) Guinness

1 cup fluffy white bread crumbs

1 cup all-purpose flour

2 teaspoons ground cinnamon

1 teaspoon allspice

continued

½ teaspoon freshly grated nutmeg

½ teaspoon ground cloves

½ teaspoon ground ginger

1 cup (2 sticks) butter, softened

4 eggs, lightly beaten

1 small apple, peeled, cored, and shredded

½ cup sliced almonds

Brandy for drizzling (optional)

Lightly sweetened whipped cream, flavored with brandy (if you like), for serving

1. Put the sugar, the orange and lemon zest, and all the dried fruit, candied cherries, and candied peel in a large bowl and pour the bottle of Guinness over everything, stirring to combine. Cover the bowl with a plate and leave it to sit overnight at room temperature.

2. The next day, in another large bowl, combine the bread crumbs and flour with all the spices. Add the butter and either cut it in with a pastry cutter, or do as traditional Irish cooks do and rub it in with your fingers. (This *does* work well, but I highly recommend taking off your rings first!)

3. Stir the eggs, grated apple, and almonds into the fruit and Guinness, then pour the wet ingredients into the dry ingredients and stir to combine. (This is when you invite everyone to take a few stirs for luck.)

4. Grease a large pudding bowl with butter. You probably don't have a pudding bowl, per se, but a 2-quart Pyrex—or other heatproof—bowl is ideal. Pour in the pudding mixture and cover the top with parchment paper and foil, making a pleat in the middle for expansion and pressing it down tightly around the rim. Tie a couple of rounds of kitchen string under the rim and fashion a handle by tying a couple more pieces of string across the top, leaving enough slack that you can use it to pick up the bowl if necessary. (More important than picking it up is the extra insurance that the top will stay on while the pudding boils.) Modern plastic pudding bowls have a fitted lid, but I don't love boiling plastic, even the heatproof kind, for 3 hours when there's something I'm going to eat inside.

5. Put the heatproof bowl in the bottom of a large stockpot and pour in water to come a little more than halfway up the sides of the bowl. Put it on the stove, bring the water to a boil over medium heat, and simmer gently for 3 hours, topping up the water from time to time. It helps to drop a few glass marbles or small round pebbles in the water—as the water gets low, they'll rattle around to alert you to add more water.

6. After 3 hours, you can either lift out the pudding with your improvised handle (be careful!) or, better, let the pudding cool in the water and then lift it out.

7. Take off the wrapping and, if you like, poke a few holes in the top with a skewer and drizzle a few tablespoons of brandy over the pudding. Cover it up with fresh parchment and foil and refrigerate until Christmas Day. (In the British Isles, it would be left on a high shelf in the pantry, but they generally keep their houses cooler than Americans do, so we're better off refrigerating the pudding to avoid any risk of mold.) If you're "feeding" your pudding with brandy, drizzle on a little more every week. You can store your pudding for a good month or more before Christmas.

8. When you're ready to serve, reboil the pudding as above for 1 hour, to heat it through. (I've heard that you can remove the foil and microwave it on medium for half an hour, but I've never done it myself; no reason why it shouldn't work, though.) Turn the pudding out, rounded side up, onto a serving platter. Heat a little brandy, maybe ⅓ cup, briefly in a small saucepan (cold brandy won't light, no matter how many matches you hold to the surface), then set it alight with a match, pour the burning liquid over the pudding, and carry it, flaming, to the table. The liquor quickly burns itself out, but the show is incomparable! Slice up the warm pudding and top each piece with a dollop of cold, lightly sweetened whipped cream, with or without brandy flavoring.

Swedish Christmas Buns

I grew up absolutely enchanted with the Swedish tradition of Saint Lucia Day. On December 13, early in the morning, the oldest daughter (that was me!) of the family dons a white robe and a crown of lit candles, and carries Saint Lucia buns, or lussekatter—*Lucia's cats—to all the sleepers in the house. I was fascinated with photos of the blond girls who serenely wore their wreaths of burning tapers while carting around trays of fresh buns. But my mother was not so keen on open flame near my head, so I was never, no, not ever, allowed to dress up like a real Swedish girl. But we did make these buns.*

¼ teaspoon saffron

1 teaspoon ground cardamom

1 cup milk

½ cup (1 stick) butter

½ cup sugar, plus more for sprinkling

1 package active dry yeast (2¼ teaspoons)

4½ cups all-purpose flour

1 teaspoon salt

3 eggs

2 teaspoons vanilla extract

½ cup golden raisins

1 tablespoon cold water

1. Cook the saffron, cardamom, and milk in a small saucepan over medium heat just until bubbles start to rise. Remove the pan from the heat, add the butter, and set aside, stirring a couple of times. Let it cool to 115°F. (If the mixture is any hotter, it may kill your yeast.)

2. Stir in the sugar and yeast, and let the mixture sit for 5 minutes, until frothy. Pour it into the bowl of a stand mixer fitted with a dough hook and beat in 3 cups of the flour on low speed. Mix in the salt, 2 eggs, and the vanilla. Separate the third egg, setting the white aside, and mix the yolk into the dough. Add the remaining flour, and continue mixing for 5 to 6 minutes, until the dough pulls away from the side of the bowl. Turn it out and knead in the raisins. Lightly grease the inside of the bowl with vegetable oil. Return the dough to the bowl and turn it so oil coats both sides. Cover with plastic wrap and let the dough rise in a warm, draft-free place until nearly doubled, about 1½ hours.

3. Preheat the oven to 375°F. Turn the dough out onto a lightly floured work surface and divide into 12 pieces. Roll each piece of dough into a round bun and set on a lightly buttered baking sheet. Cover loosely with plastic wrap and let rise for 20 to 30 minutes, until puffy.

4. Whisk the reserved egg white with the water and brush each roll. Sprinkle lightly with sugar. Bake the buns for 18 to 20 minutes, until they're golden brown.

Coconut Ice

Makes 3 dozen pieces

I've never been to Australia, though I pride myself that over the years I've done my best to contribute to the economic success of their wine industry. (And a big shout-out to you, too, New Zealand!) In addition to their wine, I've also been fascinated by Australia's emergence as a foodie hotspot, and much of what I know I've learned from food impresario Donna Hay; I love her approach to fresh, pure, and exciting flavors without a lot of fuss. My version of coconut ice is based on hers. It's a sort of creamy coconut fudge that's a big favorite Down Under at holiday time, which, since their weather is essentially opposite to that of the northern hemisphere, they celebrate in swimsuits on the beach. What a country!

4 cups confectioners' sugar

2 cups coconut flakes, plus 2 to 3 tablespoons more for sprinkling

1 can (14 ounces) sweetened condensed milk

1 teaspoon vanilla extract

2 to 3 drops liquid food coloring (any color you like)

1. Line an 8-inch square pan with foil, letting a couple of inches hang over the side for easy lifting later on.

2. Put the sugar, coconut, condensed milk, and vanilla into a bowl and stir to combine.

3. Put half the mixture into the prepared pan, pressing it into a smooth, even layer. Add a few drops of food coloring to the remaining mixture in the bowl to make a pale pastel color (pink is traditional). Press this colored layer gently over the first, smoothing until it is even.

4. Sprinkle a few tablespoons of additional coconut over the top and press it gently into the surface with your fingertips. Freeze the pan for 2 hours, until the coconut ice is very firm. To serve, remove it from the pan using the foil handles and cut it into 36 squares. Store it in an airtight container in the freezer for a week.

Moravian Sugar Cake

generous cooks use their thumbs to poke holes in the dough   *Makes a 9-by-13-inch cake*

This is not solely a Christmas dish—in fact, Easter in Winston-Salem, NC is unimaginable without it—and most people tend to buy their sugar cake ready-made from Dewey's, an old bakery in Winston-Salem, or the Winkler Bakery on Main Street in Old Salem, a charmingly low-key restored settlement. Old Salem is well worth a visit, especially at the holidays to partake in the quaint custom of a "lovefeast," an evening carol service where participants hold aloft a beeswax candle wrapped in a red paper frill and finish with a feast of buns and coffee. Lovefeast or no, hardly anyone leaves Old Salem without a slab of this cake in hand, and we love to eat it Christmas morning, no matter what else we're having!

FOR THE CAKE:

½ cup milk

¼ cup (½ stick) butter, softened

1 package active dry yeast (2¼ teaspoons)

5 tablespoons sugar

2 eggs

¼ teaspoon salt

1 medium russet potato, cooked and mashed, or ½ cup leftover mashed potatoes

3½ to 4 cups all-purpose flour

FOR THE TOPPING:

6 tablespoons (¾ stick) butter

1 cup light brown sugar

½ teaspoon ground cinnamon

¼ teaspoon freshly grated nutmeg

1. Warm the milk and butter in a small saucepan over medium heat until the butter melts. Remove the pan from the heat and cool the milk mixture to 115°F. (If the mixture is any hotter, it may kill your yeast.) Stir in 1 tablespoon of the sugar and the yeast and let it sit for 5 minutes until frothy.

2. Pour the milk into a stand mixer fitted with a dough hook, add the remaining sugar, eggs, salt, and potato, and mix. Add the flour, a little at a time, up to 3 ½ cups. Don't add any more unless the dough is very wet, and then only add it a few tablespoons at a time. The dough should be soft.

3. Lightly butter a 9-by-13-inch glass baking dish and turn the dough into it, pressing gently to spread it. Cover it with plastic wrap and let it rise in a warm, draft-free place until doubled, about 1 hour.

continued

4. When you're ready to bake, preheat the oven to 375°F and put all the topping ingredients in a small saucepan over medium heat. Cook, stirring, just until the butter melts and then remove the pan from the heat. Poke the dough all over with a fingertip. (Legend holds that generous cooks use their thumb, those less so use the small end of a wooden spoon!) Be sure to make holes right up to the edge of the pan.

5. Pour the topping mixture over the surface of the cake so that it drips down into all the holes. Bake for 15 to 18 minutes, until the cake is golden and the topping is bubbling. You can serve the cake warm or at room temperature, but it's best eaten the day it's made.

Swedish Rice Pudding

the almond means good luck   *Makes 6 to 8 servings*

So I never got to play Saint Lucia (see page 140). At least we always had Swedish rice pudding on Christmas Eve. The regular long-grain rice that's likely in your cupboard will make rice pudding, but it won't be nearly as good as the kind you can make if you look for a short- or medium-grain rice. In fact, one of the best ways to ensure a good outcome is to use Arborio, Carnaroli, or another short-grain risotto rice. These cook up creamy and tender, giving their starch off into the sauce but remaining whole and separate. Let the pudding cook low and slow so you don't form a skin on top. This should be a particularly creamy dish. A whole almond is supposed to be slipped into the pudding, and whoever gets it in their serving is, by tradition, meant to be married the coming year. In our house, we said whoever got the almond got good luck, and great was the digging around with the spoon while we tried to feel for that almond. After a while, my mother just gave up and put in one almond for each kid to cut down on the accusations and recriminations. Ah, Christmas memories! The mild pudding is good with a dollop of lingonberry jam on top (or raspberry or other red jam if you can't find lingonberry).

- 2 cups half-and-half or light cream
- 2 cups whole milk
- ½ cup sugar
- 1 egg, lightly beaten
- 1 teaspoon vanilla extract
- ½ teaspoon ground cardamom
- ½ teaspoon ground cinnamon
- ¾ cup raw short-grain rice
- 1 whole blanched almond (or more as needed)

1. Preheat the oven to 325°F and lightly butter a 2-quart casserole dish. In a large bowl, whisk together everything but the rice and almond. Stir in the rice and pour the mixture into the prepared dish. Drop the almond into the pudding and cover the casserole with a lid or foil.

2. Set the casserole dish inside a 9-by-13-inch baking dish. Put the whole thing in the oven and pour hot water into the larger dish to halfway up the sides of the smaller dish.

3. Bake the pudding for 1 to 1½ hours, until it looks creamy. Remove it carefully from the oven (it's easiest and safest to lift the pudding dish out of the hot water and let the hot water stay in the oven to cool before removing it). Serve the rice pudding warm or cool.

Turrones (Christmas Nougat)

addictively chewy and delicious   *Makes about 1 pound*

There are variations on nougat—torron, turron, torone—all around Spain, Italy, and in Catalonian parts of southern France, and the age-old candy-making tradition has spread to different parts of the world. No Cuban Christmas dinner is complete without a plate of this chewy nougat made from toasted nuts, honey, and egg whites. The Cuban version is almost always the soft, chewy style, rather than the crisp, crackling Alicante style that is popular in Spain, so don't expect this to set up hard. I'm warning you, it's got the potential to be a sticky mess, so make sure your candy thermometer is calibrated properly and use a stand mixer if you can. It's crucial to beat it for 10 minutes, until it stiffens.

Traditionally, the nougat is poured into molds lined with edible rice paper, which is also very useful for another deliciously sticky mess, Italian Chocolate Panforte, on page 154, so if you can source some at an Asian market or baking supply store, you'll find some other uses for it. Otherwise, line a dish with parchment paper.

The nuts are typically left whole for the best-looking presentation. It doesn't matter whether you use blanched almonds or no; in fact, the skins look rather nice against the pale nougat, as does the gleam of green from the pistachios, but it's best to remove the skins from the hazelnuts since those tend to be tougher. The pistachios are not traditional in Cuba, though you see them in European versions of this candy; if you like, leave them out and simply increase the amounts of the other nuts.

Edible rice paper or parchment paper

¾ cup whole pistachios, without shells

¾ cup whole almonds, without shells

¾ cup whole hazelnuts, without shells, skins removed (see Homemade Chocolate-Hazelnut Spread, page 163)

2½ cups sugar

¼ cup honey

¼ cup light corn syrup

2 egg whites

1 teaspoon vanilla extract

⅛ teaspoon salt

1. Butter the bottom of a 9-inch square pan and line the bottom with rice paper or parchment paper. If you use parchment, butter the top side of it, too.

2. In a large dry skillet over medium heat, toss the nuts for 2 to 3 minutes, just until they smell fragrant and toasty. Pour them out of the hot pan into a bowl and set them aside.

3. Put the sugar, honey, corn syrup and ¼ cup water in a heavy-bottomed saucepan over medium-high heat and bring the mixture to a boil, stirring just to dissolve the sugar. Affix a candy thermometer to the pot and let the mixture cook until it reaches 300°F (hard-crack stage).

4. While the sugar is boiling, beat the egg whites with a hand or stand mixer until they are stiff but not dry.

5. With the beaters running, slowly drizzle the hot sugar syrup into the egg whites and continue to beat on medium speed for 10 minutes until the mixture starts to stiffen. With the mixer on low, add the nuts, vanilla, and salt.

6. Quickly spread the nougat in the prepared pan, pressing it down with buttered fingers to smooth the surface, and allow it to rest overnight. (If you have enough rice paper, you can press a second layer on top. Otherwise, just let the nougat air-dry.) To serve, cut it into narrow fingers.

Tiny Mince Pies with Phyllo

crisp, crackly, and spicy   *Makes 2 dozen tarts*

You do not have to make mincemeat to make a mincemeat pie. Even ordinary American supermarkets stock jars or Tetrapak boxes of mincemeat around Christmastime. Buy the base ready-made and then dress it up by adding goodies such as extra orange zest and juice, along with some additional dried fruit, such as cherries or cranberries, for a tart burst of chewiness. And although it would be nice, of course, to make a buttery homemade short-crust pastry to encase it, it's also a lot easier to thaw out a roll of phyllo dough and use that instead. That way, you can have wonderful pastries that, for all intents and purposes, are homemade, with a lot less fuss.

Double check the mincemeat you buy and make sure you've got 2 cups of actual mincemeat! Some of the packages of mincemeat are intended to be reconstituted with water or orange juice, so if the mincemeat seems dry and crumbly, make sure you follow the package instructions so you're starting with 2 cups of "finished" mincemeat before you add any additional ingredients.

These make excellent teeny-tiny mince pies as well; just cut the phyllo smaller to fit into mini muffin tins.

2 cups mincemeat
¼ cup dried cherries or cranberries
Grated zest and juice of 1 orange
¼ teaspoon ground cloves
17 ounces frozen phyllo pastry, thawed
½ cup (1 stick) butter, melted
Confectioners' sugar, for garnish
Whipped cream, for serving

1. Preheat the oven to 375°F and lightly grease two 12-cup muffin tins. Put the mincemeat in a bowl and stir in the dried cherries, orange zest and juice, and cloves.

2. Lay a sheet of phyllo on a clean work surface, and cover the remaining phyllo with a clean dampened dish towel to keep it from drying out. Using a pastry brush, brush melted butter on the sheet and continue layering and brushing with butter until you have 8 sheets stacked up. Cut the stack into 6 squares, then push a buttered, stacked square down into a muffin cup, letting the edges stand upright. Repeat with more phyllo until all the muffin tins are filled.

3. Put a heaping tablespoon of mincemeat down into the center of each phyllo-lined cup. Bake for 20 to 22 minutes, until the mincemeat is bubbling and the phyllo is golden brown and crisp.

4. When all the mincemeat tarts are baked, sieve confectioners' sugar generously over them and serve them warm, dropping a spoonful of whipped cream on top of each just before it's going to be eaten (if you let it sit, the cream will melt and the phyllo won't be crisp!).

Dutch Christmas Bread

"bread" is way too ordinary to describe it

Makes 1 large loaf

We have some really lovely Dutch friends, Akkie and Els, from the north of Holland, where Akkie used to be the head of a big technical college. One holiday season, Akkie brought us a large and elaborate braided bread that had been baked by students at his school. It was covered with white icing and studded with candied fruit and sliced almonds, and when cut open, it revealed a tunnel of rich, moist handmade marzipan. "Is this stollen?" we asked in wonder as we stuffed it into our faces. "No, no," he said. "This, this is Christmas bread."

½ cup milk

½ cup (1 stick) butter

¼ cup granulated sugar

1 package active dry yeast (2¼ teaspoons)

1 egg

2½ cups all-purpose flour

½ teaspoon salt

½ cup golden raisins

½ cup candied orange peel (see Pamelas, page 35, to make your own)

1 tube (7 ounces) almond paste

½ cup confectioners' sugar, plus additional for dusting (optional)

1 to 2 tablespoons orange juice

2 tablespoons sliced, toasted almonds (optional)

1. Heat the milk and butter in a microwave for 1 minute. Stir and microwave for another 10 to 20 seconds if necessary to melt the butter. Let cool to to 115°F. (If the mixture is any hotter, it may kill your yeast.) Stir in the sugar and yeast and allow it to sit for 10 minutes until foamy.

2. Pour the milk and butter into the bowl of a stand mixer fitted with a dough hook. Add the egg, mix it in, then gradually beat in the flour and salt. Continue to mix for 5 to 6 minutes, until smooth and elastic.

3. When the dough pulls away from the sides of the bowl in a soft, smooth mass, add the raisins and candied peel and continue to mix to distribute them throughout. Turn the dough out of the bowl and grease the bowl with vegetable oil. Return the dough to the bowl and flip it to coat all sides lightly with oil. Cover it and let it rest in a warm, draft-free place until it has doubled in size, about 1½ hours.

4. Turn the dough out onto a clean, lightly floured work surface. Shape it into an oval 14 inches long. Knead the almond paste on a clean work surface until it's pliable. Roll it into a log about 12 inches

continued

long and lay it along the dough about a third of the way from one of the long sides. Fold the other side over the marzipan, not letting the edges meet up exactly but leaving a 1-inch edge of dough uncovered.

5. Lightly grease a baking sheet and delicately transfer the dough onto it. Cover it loosely with plastic wrap and let it rise for 30 minutes while you preheat the oven to 350°F.

6. Bake the bread for 40 to 45 minutes, checking it now and then. If it seems to be browning too fast, cover it loosely with aluminum foil.

7. Allow the bread to cool completely. Combine the confectioners' sugar with the orange juice to make a thick icing. Spread it over the top of the bread and sprinkle it with almonds and additional confectioners' sugar, if desired.

Buñuelos

These little doughnut sticks are a necessity on the Mexican Christmas table, but they are eaten, in one form or another, round or long, all around South America and the world, sometimes stuffed, sometimes drizzled with syrup or covered in confectioners' sugar.

2½ cups all-purpose flour, plus more for kneading

½ cup light brown sugar

1 teaspoon baking powder

½ teaspoon salt

½ cup milk

2 eggs

¼ cup (½ stick) butter, melted

Vegetable oil, for frying

½ cup granulated sugar

1½ teaspoons ground cinnamon

1. In a large bowl, whisk together the flour, brown sugar, baking powder, and salt. Make a well in the center and pour in the milk, eggs, and melted butter; stir to combine.

2. Turn out the dough onto a lightly floured surface and knead it with your palms a few times until it's smooth and workable. Divide it into 24 pieces and roll each piece into a narrow rope about 6 inches long (it will contract in the hot oil).

3. Let the doughnuts rest while you heat 3 inches of vegetable oil in a deep, heavy-bottomed saucepan over medium-high heat. Affix a candy or frying thermometer to the side of the pot and heat the oil to 350°F. Fry the buñuelos in batches until they are golden brown, 2 to 3 minutes per side. Drain them on paper towels.

4. Combine the sugar and cinnamon in a shallow bowl and toss each doughnut in it while it's still hot. Serve the buñuelos right away.

Italian Chocolate Panforte

more candy than cake

Makes an 8-inch cake

Panforte has roots dating back to the Middle Ages, when this "strong bread," as literally translated, would keep for a long time, making it suitable for travel to the Crusades or perhaps less far afield. It survives today, a thin and potent cake with the strong spicing of medieval times intact, along with the taste for dried fruit that our ancestors developed since no other fruit was available to them in the cold months. It's kind of difficult to give your kids a history lesson on how hard people used to have it in the old days when you're feeding them this incredibly pleasing holiday confection.

To make it as authentic as possible, you're supposed to line the pan with edible rice paper, which is kind of like parchment paper that you eat; it can be sliced and consumed with the cake. You'll find it in baking supply stores and also in Asian markets. If you can't get it, parchment paper is the next best option, but make sure not to eat it! This is an amazingly sticky cake, and anything else will make a mess of it! Tightly wrapped, the cake can keep for many months, but it's unlikely it will hang around that long.

Edible rice paper or parchment paper
½ cup sugar
¾ cup honey
1 cup chopped hazelnuts
1 cup chopped almonds
½ cup candied orange peel (see Pamelas, page 35, to make your own)
½ cup dried cranberries
1 teaspoon ground cinnamon
¼ teaspoon ground cloves
¼ teaspoon freshly ground nutmeg
¼ teaspoon freshly ground black pepper
½ cup all-purpose flour
4 ounces bittersweet chocolate
Unsweetened cocoa powder, for dusting

1. Preheat the oven to 300°F. Cut the edible rice paper (or parchment paper) to fit the bottom of an 8-inch round cake tin.

2. Put the sugar and honey in a small saucepan over medium heat and bring the mixture to a boil, stirring to dissolve the sugar. Clip on a candy thermometer and cook until it reaches the soft-ball stage, 240°F, 8 to 10 minutes.

3. While the honey boils, combine the nuts, candied peel, cranberries, spices (including pepper), and flour in a mixing bowl. Break the chocolate into a large microwavable bowl, microwave on

sweet christmas 154

high for 1 minute, and then stir vigorously with a fork. If you need more heat, microwave in 10-second bursts, stirring after each, until the chocolate is smooth.

4. When the honey reaches 240°F, remove the pot from the heat. Scrape the melted chocolate into it and stir to combine. Pour the nut and fruit mixture into the pot and stir quickly to mix together. It will get very stiff fast. Scrape the mixture into the prepared pan on top of the edible rice paper. A heatproof silicone scraper or spatula is ideal for this. Smooth the top until it's even.

5. Bake the panforte for 30 minutes, then let it cool for 20 minutes in the pan before gently lifting it out using a knife or offset spatula. When the panforte is completely cool, dust the top liberally with cocoa. Wrap it in plastic and store it at room temperature. To serve, cut it into narrow wedges with a sharp kitchen knife.

British Christmas Cake

Making the Christmas cake is no joke to the British. They begin both the plum pudding and the cake months before the holidays in order to let them develop complex and layered flavors. And it's true, a heavy-duty fruitcake that has been aged for three or four weeks (or, heaven help us, months) and carefully "fed" with a little brandy or whiskey now and then will indeed have a deeper, richer flavor than one that was made a few days ago. But it doesn't necessarily follow that the fruitcake made a few days before being cut will taste bad! The Christmas cake ingredients may seem similar to the pudding, but the result is very different. It's a dark golden cake densely packed with dried fruit and topped with a layer of marzipan that is itself topped with royal icing, which hardens and keeps the marzipan and cake beneath soft and tender. The cake is usually cut on Christmas Day, but the real eating takes place over the next twelve days, until the "Twelfth Day of Christmas," which is January 6. The final day is known in Ireland as "Little Christmas" or—my favorite—as "Women's Christmas," since in the old days it was the one day of the year when the man of the house was supposed to do the cooking!

2 cups golden raisins

1 cup dark raisins

1 cup currants

1 cup candied cherries, halved

½ cup candied orange peel, chopped (see Pamelas, page 35, to make your own)

½ teaspoon ground cinnamon

½ teaspoon ground ginger

¼ teaspoon ground cloves

¼ teaspoon freshly grated nutmeg

1 teaspoon vanilla extract

Grated zest and juice of 1 lemon

Grated zest and juice of 1 orange

¼ cup whiskey, plus more for drizzling

1 cup (2 sticks) butter, softened

1 cup light brown sugar

4 eggs

1 cup ground almonds

2 cups all-purpose flour

1 teaspoon baking powder

½ teaspoon salt

Confectioners' sugar (optional)

1 tube (7 ounces) marzipan (optional)

2 recipes Royal Icing (optional; see Gingerbread People, page 44)

1. In a large bowl, combine all the dried fruit with the spices, vanilla, and the zest and juice of the orange and lemon. Stir in the whiskey. Cover the mixture with a plate or plastic wrap and leave it to soak overnight.

2. The next day, when you're ready to bake, preheat the oven to 300°F. Butter the bottom of a large, deep (6-inch) cake tin and line it with a circle of parchment, buttering the top of the paper, too.

3. Cream the butter and brown sugar until fluffy in a large bowl with an electric mixer. Add the eggs one at a time, beating well after each, then beat in the ground almonds.

4. Using a large wooden spoon (not the mixer), stir in the flour, baking powder, and salt. Add the fruit and all the liquid in the bowl and stir to combine. Turn the batter into the prepared pan and smooth the top. It will be quite thick.

5. Cover the pan with a layer of parchment paper and seal it with foil. This will keep the cake from burning during the long cooking time. Bake it for 3 hours, then lift off the foil and insert a skewer to test it. If the center is still wet, cover it again with the parchment and foil and bake for another 30 to 60 minutes, or until the skewer comes out clean. Let the cake cool overnight in the cake pan.

6. The next day, gently run a knife around the outside edge and carefully turn the cake out of the pan. Poke holes all over the bottom with a skewer and drizzle a few tablespoons of whiskey into it. Wrap the whole cake in parchment paper and then foil. Keep it in the back of the refrigerator, adding a little more whiskey every week until Christmas (you can keep this up for 2 months, or you can make the cake and just age it for a few days).

7. If you don't want to frost the cake, you can serve it as is, or you can give it a heavy dusting of confectioners' sugar. To frost the cake, at least 2 days before you plan to eat it, knead the marzipan with your hands to soften it. Sprinkle a clean work surface thickly with confectioners' sugar and roll the marzipan out into a large circle. Roll it loosely around the rolling pin and lift it onto the cake, opening it over the top and sides and folding and molding it with your hands to fit it all around the cake.

8. Make the royal icing and spread it thickly over the marzipan. Leave it to dry, uncovered, for a couple of days. The icing makes an airtight seal that lets the marzipan sort of melt into the sides of the cake. It's usual to top the cake with silly Christmas figures, such as a little plastic Santa and a sleigh, or some tiny green Christmas trees and a few reindeer.

9. To serve, cut off a quarter of the cake and slice that into "fingers" about 1-inch thick. Wrap the cake tightly in plastic after cutting it.

Pink Grapefruit Marmalade page 164

Homemade Chocolate-Hazelnut Spread page 163

Hot Fudge Sauce page 165

CHAPTER EIGHT

Homemade Gifts to Give

❋

All Wrapped Up and Somewhere to Go

There's nothing in this chapter that you wouldn't happily make and keep to eat all by yourself, but everything in here also makes a particularly nice food gift. There's something to suit all kinds of tastes, from a jar of homemade Chocolate-Hazelnut Spread or a truly beautiful, faintly pink Grapefruit Marmalade (and who knew how easy and delicious *that* could be?) to the most sublime and simple Dark Chocolate Truffles imaginable. There are also some sharp and spicy Spicy Cheddar Coins, the ubiquitous holiday gift throughout the South, as well as some more unusual treats to surprise and impress your friends, among them, truffles made from chocolate and leftover fruitcake. (According to some pundits, that's the only kind of fruitcake there is! If you're in that camp, this recipe might change your mind.)

Once you've baked or cooked, don't make yourself crazy with packaging. A simple box or bag, a bow, and a handwritten card or label is pretty much all you need to show that you made the effort. And in our society of excess buying and collecting of unneeded stuff, your friends and family may be more pleased and delighted than you can even imagine to receive something small, thoughtful, and delicious that can be consumed and enjoyed without needing to be stored or kept or displayed. It's a gift that truly is all about the thought (and the flavor) and might turn out to be the most welcome of all this holiday.

White Chocolate–Peppermint Hot Cocoa Mix

mix it up with a peppermint stick   *Makes about 4 cups mix, enough for 16 mugs of cocoa*

A jar of this luxurious hot chocolate mix is the gift that keeps on giving all winter. Once you get the hang of the proportions for making homemade mix, you can vary it with any flavors you like, from dark cocoa powder to the decidedly grown-up choice of a hint of cayenne, which brings out the nuances of the cocoa. And you'll never go back to store-bought mixes again. Serve each mug with a peppermint stick for stirring.

2½ cups nonfat dry milk powder

¾ cup sugar

½ cup unsweetened cocoa powder

½ cup white chocolate chips

¾ cup mini marshmallows

16 peppermint sticks

1. Combine all the ingredients except the peppermint sticks in a large, tightly lidded glass jar.

2. To make a cup of cocoa, put ¼ cup of the mixture in a mug, making sure there are some chips and marshmallows in each mug. Top this with ¾ cup of boiling water. Stir well with a peppermint stick, and sip slowly.

Dark Chocolate Truffles

rich ganache dipped in even more chocolate   *Makes about 4 dozen truffles*

If you've ever wondered what you might do with gourmet bars of specialty chocolate—besides unwrapping and snarfing them—here is the answer. This is the simplest, most basic recipe for a rich, dark chocolate truffle. Once you've mastered it—which you can do in one candy-making session—you'll be known far and wide for your chocolate skills. Since these are so simple, it certainly helps to buy very good chocolate; I like to splurge and get Callebaut or Valrhona. But it can't be denied that you can also get extremely good results with supermarket chocolate, such as my old favorite, Ghirardelli's 70% cacao. You can experiment with adding a little flavoring once you get the hang of the basic recipe. Try a tablespoon or two of Chambord or Grand Marnier, or infuse a large sprig of fresh mint leaves or a bag of Earl Gray tea leaves in the hot cream for 15 minutes, removing it just before adding the chocolate.

⅔ cup whipping cream

8 ounces good-quality dark chocolate

1 cup unsweetened cocoa powder

1. Bring the cream just to a boil in a saucepan. Immediately remove it from the heat and break the chocolate pieces into the hot cream. Stir gently to melt them.

2. Scrape the mixture into a bowl and let it stand in a cool place until firm, 1 to 2 hours. If the temperature in your kitchen is very warm, you can put it in the refrigerator, but check it every 5 minutes or so and don't let it chill into complete stiffness. It should still be pliable.

3. Line a baking sheet with parchment paper. Use a pair of small teaspoons (or your buttered hands) to form the chocolate mixture into very small balls, no larger than about ¾ inch, and deposit them on the parchment paper, smoothing the edges with your fingertips without overworking the chocolate.

4. Put the cocoa in a shallow bowl. Working in batches, toss the truffles gently in the cocoa. Store them in an airtight container in the refrigerator for up to 2 weeks. You can toss them again in cocoa just before serving. (They also look nice set into individual mini cupcake papers.)

Homemade Chocolate-Hazelnut Spread

My kids love that Nutella TV commercial where a mom earnestly assures us that feeding her kids Nutella means they get a healthy and nutritious breakfast that they love every day. My sugar-loving sons are like, "Pleeeease?" I'm all for Nutella, and even more in favor of the homemade kind because it's so good, but I'm not kidding myself that it's health food! We'll stick with the whole-grain toast and the unsweetened peanut butter for every day, but now and then, as a treat, this is sheer bliss. I use a neutral-flavored oil such as vegetable or canola, but if you have pure hazelnut oil (which costs a small fortune, so I don't!), this is the place to use it. Adding both cocoa and melted chocolate makes this version super tasty, and a little milk helps make it creamy and smooth. This recipe makes two jars: one to keep and one to give to a very good friend.

> 2 cups hazelnuts, without shells
>
> 3 tablespoons vegetable oil
>
> ⅓ cup unsweetened cocoa powder
>
> 1½ cups confectioners' sugar
>
> ¼ cup whole milk
>
> 1 teaspoon vanilla extract
>
> ½ teaspoon salt, or to taste
>
> 1 cup (6 ounces) semisweet chocolate chips

1. Preheat the oven to 400°F. Put the hazelnuts on a rimmed baking sheet and toast them for 10 minutes, until they're lightly browned, shaking the pan once or twice. Cool them for 10 minutes.

2. Put the hazelnuts on a dish towel spread out on a clean work surface. Fold the towel over the nuts and rub vigorously to remove the husks. Lift the naked nuts into the bowl of a food processor. Process them for 2 to 3 minutes, until they're ground, then add the oil and continue to process until you have a smooth paste. This could take up to 5 minutes.

3. Add the cocoa, confectioners' sugar, milk, vanilla, and salt, and continue to process for another 1 to 2 minutes to combine.

4. Melt the chocolate in a small bowl in the microwave, heating it for about 1 minute on high, then stirring well. If necessary, heat it in additional 10-second bursts, stirring after each, until it becomes smooth. Scrape the melted chocolate into the food processor and pulse until the mixture is combined. Taste and add a pinch more salt if needed.

5. Spoon the spread into two 1-cup jars and seal them. Store them in the refrigerator for up to 3 weeks.

Pink Grapefruit Marmalade

If you're not a marmalade eater, it's probably because you remember a bitter and surprising childhood experience: you were expecting the overwhelming sweetness of something like grape jelly, and you got something . . . very different. Try this version with your adult taste buds. The tart, sharp flavor of a good, sweet pink grapefruit serves as the perfect counterpoint to the sugar, and the lemon adds a layer of complexity and brightness. The finished marmalade is a delicate, rose-pink color, and it glows like a jewel in the jar. You'll have to make a second batch if you're planning to use this as a gift because you won't want to give it all away! (But don't double this recipe; it works best in these proportions.)

> 3 medium pink grapefruits
> 5 lemons
> 7 cups sugar

1. Use a vegetable peeler to carefully separate the rind from the fruit of the grapefruits and lemons, peeling off just the zest and avoiding the bitter white pith beneath. Chop the rind into narrow strips and place it in a large saucepan.

2. Use a sharp knife to slice the pith off the fruit. Then chop the fruit and put it and the juice in the pan, discarding the pith, seeds, and chunks of membrane.

3. Add 10 cups of water and bring the mixture to a boil. Reduce the heat and cook for 1 hour, until the marmalade is reduced by about half.

4. Add the sugar to the pan and cook, stirring, until it dissolves. Put a candy thermometer in the pan and boil the mixture until it reaches 222°F, about 15 minutes.

5. Remove the pan from the heat. Cool the marmalade for an hour, then spoon it into clean half-pint jars. Cool it completely before screwing on the lids. Store it in the refrigerator for up to 4 weeks.

Hot Fudge Sauce

Makes about 2 ½ cups sauce

You can make hot fudge sauce with melted chocolate that's got a rich and intense flavor, but that kind tends to firm up as soon as it hits the ice cream. I myself am more fond of the kind that stays liquid and hot, dripping down the sides of your scoop of ice cream to make a warm puddle around the edges. For that, you need unsweetened cocoa. With the richness of the butter and cream, it doesn't really matter if you use the most ordinary supermarket cocoa here—it will still be delicious, especially when it's reheated just before serving. You may think that adding a teaspoon of vanilla is unnecessary in such a deep, dark confection, but it rounds out the flavor, and you'd miss it if it wasn't there. The sauce will firm a little but still stay soft in the refrigerator, so you can dip up a surreptitious spoonful now and then, directly from the jar.

I cup whipping cream

½ cup (I stick) butter

I cup dark brown sugar

½ cup granulated sugar

I cup unsweetened cocoa powder

I teaspoon vanilla extract

1. Put the cream and butter in a large, heavy saucepan over medium heat. Add the sugars and cook the mixture, stirring frequently, until they are dissolved. Simmer the liquid for 2 to 3 minutes, stirring occasionally, until it has thickened slightly.

2. Whisk in the cocoa and cook for another minute. Remove the pan from the heat and stir in the vanilla. Serve the sauce immediately or store it in an airtight jar in the refrigerator for up to 2 weeks. The sauce can be gently reheated before serving.

Salted Caramel Sauce

Makes about 1 ½ cups sauce

The words "salted caramel" make a lot of people start to drool. For anyone who ever loved potato chips and chocolate together, the salted caramel craze takes that flavor obsession of salty and sweet to the ultimate heights. Long may this particular food fad live on! Unlike store-bought caramel sauces, which tend to have a one-note flavor—very sweet—this one has mellow depth, sweetness, and complexity from the homemade caramel, the salty butter, and the hint of vanilla. Don't be tempted to increase the vanilla. You want a delicate hint, not an overwhelming top note. Kids don't love alcohol in their desserts, to put it mildly, but if you were making this for adults only, I would highly recommend stirring a tablespoon or two of bourbon into the jug of warm sauce right before giving it to guests to pour over individual bowls of vanilla ice cream.

1 cup sugar
½ cup (1 stick) butter
½ cup whipping cream
¼ teaspoon vanilla extract
¼ teaspoon kosher or flaky sea salt

1. Put the sugar in the bottom of a large, heavy saucepan over medium-high heat and pour in ⅓ cup of water slowly. Without stirring but watching all the time, heat the pan until the sugar melts and starts to brown. When it does, swirl the pan very gently to let the mixture brown evenly. (If you stir the sugar before it melts, you'll push sugar crystals up the sides of the pan, and later these may cause your beautiful caramel to abruptly crystallize again.)

2. Cook the caramel for 5 to 7 minutes, until it's a rich, golden brown. Remove it from the heat and add the butter, stirring gently to melt it. Pour in the cream and stir to combine. Last, add the vanilla and salt.

3. Cool the sauce completely and store it in an airtight jar in the refrigerator for up to 2 weeks. It will firm up somewhat in the fridge, but you can reheat it gently to soften it before serving it again.

Pecan Snowballs

crumbly, buttery cookie balls packed with nutty flavor *Makes 4 dozen cookies*

These little white balls of cookie come in endless variations, but they usually appear under names such as Russian Teacakes and Mexican Wedding Cakes (those are two cultures not usually thought of as sharing much in the way of cuisine, no?). What stays the same recipe to recipe is the combination of some sort of finely chopped nut—the oilier, the better—flour, sugar, and plenty of butter. Rolled into small balls and then liberally coated with confectioners' sugar, they make a surprisingly elegant gift when nestled into miniature cupcake papers in a box or tin. They'll look like far more effort than you actually went to, particularly if you have a food processor. I like the mild sweetness of pecans, but you can use nearly any nut: try walnuts, almonds, even macadamias; chestnuts are particularly nice.

2 cups pecans

1 cup (2 sticks) butter, softened

1½ cups confectioners' sugar

1 teaspoon vanilla extract

2 cups all-purpose flour

¼ teaspoon baking powder

¼ teaspoon salt

¼ teaspoon freshly grated nutmeg

¼ teaspoon ground cinnamon

1. Put the pecans in the bowl of a food processor and pulse until they're finely chopped. Don't overprocess and let the nuts get warm, or the texture will be too oily.

2. Add the butter, ½ cup of the confectioners' sugar, and vanilla and continue to pulse until well mixed. Add the flour, baking powder, and salt and process just until the dough comes together in a ball. Chill it for 2 hours, until firm.

3. Preheat the oven to 350°F and lightly grease 2 baking sheets. Roll the dough into 1-inch balls and place them 1 inch apart on the baking sheets. Bake them for 10 to 12 minutes, until just starting to brown lightly. Don't overbake, or the cookies will be too crumbly.

4. Cool the cookies completely. In a gallon-size zip-top storage bag, combine the remaining confectioners' sugar with the nutmeg and cinnamon. Working in batches, put a portion of the cooled cookies in the bag and shake gently to coat them liberally with sugar. Store them in an airtight container for up to 1 week. (You may want to toss the cookies in a little more sugar just before serving them, so seal up the bag and keep any remaining sugar until needed.) If you're packing the cookies in miniature paper muffin cups, put them in the papers just before packing them. (If you store them for several days in the cups, the oil from the nuts will leach into the paper.)

Rum Balls

Children do not like rum balls (they probably shouldn't eat them, either, although the amount of alcohol in each cookie is pretty negligible). But children like very much to make rum balls, and it was always my task as a kid. My dad was an almost complete teetotaler, but he loved rum balls at Christmas, especially after the flavor had been allowed to mellow for a few days. I loved to make them and roll them in the sugar and feed them to my dad. After an initial taste, I never wanted to eat them . . . well, until I was an adult. Now my kids are the same way. Some family traditions go on and on!

- 2 loosely packed cups vanilla wafers
- 1 cup pecan halves
- 3 cups confectioners' sugar
- 1 tablespoon unsweetened cocoa powder
- ¼ cup rum or bourbon
- 1 tablespoon corn syrup

1. Put the vanilla wafers in the bowl of a food processor and pulse to form fine crumbs. Add the pecans and continue to pulse until they're finely choppped.

2. Put in 1 cup of the confectioners' sugar and the cocoa and pulse just to combine. With the machine running, pour in the rum and corn syrup and process until the mixture starts to clump together. Chill it for 1 to 2 hours, until firm.

3. Put the remaining 2 cups confectioners' sugar in a shallow bowl. Roll the cookie mixture into balls about ¾ inch in diameter (smaller is better, since they taste potent), then roll each ball liberally in the sugar. Store the rum balls in an airtight container in the refrigerator for up to 2 weeks. The flavor will mellow and improve after the first 2 days.

Christmas Cake Truffles

one more for the adults—why should kids get all the fun?

Nigella Lawson, once again, was my inspiration for these cuter-than-cute little truffles. She calls her clever originals "bonbons" and makes them out of leftover Christmas pudding and sherry, and you can certainly do that with the leftovers from the holiday pudding (from my Irish husband's family recipe, in fact, on page 137). But I've put a more American spin on them here, using a cup of chopped-up American fruitcake and some good old Kentucky bourbon, as well as upping the chocolate quotient a bit. Even if you're not familiar with the typical shape of a British Christmas pudding, you'll recognize the cuteness of these miniatures, with their topping of royal icing representing whipped cream or brandy butter and the bit of green and red signifying the traditional sprig of holly that tops a flaming plum pudding. These potent little bites are not too sweet, and they're terrific to accompany after-dinner coffee at a holiday meal.

> 6 ounces bittersweet chocolate (such as Ghirardelli's 70% cacao bar)
>
> 1 cup finely chopped or crumbled fruitcake (any fruitcake you have, or use the one on page 137)
>
> 3 tablespoons bourbon
>
> 2 tablespoons light corn syrup
>
> 1 recipe Royal Icing (page 44)
>
> Red and green gumdrops or maraschino cherries

1. Line a baking sheet with parchment paper. Melt the chocolate in a bowl in the microwave, heating it for 1 minute on high and stirring well. If you need more heat, microwave the chocolate in one or two more 10-second blasts, stirring well after each, until it is smooth. Be very careful not to overheat it.

2. Stir in the fruitcake, bourbon, and corn syrup until the mixture is well combined and finely textured. You don't want any big chunks other than bits of fruit, so press any lumps of cake against the side of the bowl with your spoon to break them up.

3. Lightly butter your hands and roll the truffle mixture into 1-inch balls, lining them up on the prepared baking sheet. Chill them for 2 hours in the refrigerator, until firm.

4. When the truffles are chilled, spread a dollop of royal icing on top of each truffle. Using a pair of kitchen shears, snip the red and green gumdrops or maraschino cherries into tiny strips. Press a couple of green strips on top of the icing, to represent holly leaves, and add a couple of red bits to represent holly berries. Return the truffles to the fridge to firm up, then store them in an airtight container in the refrigerator for up to 2 weeks. The flavor will mellow and improve after the first day or two.

Spicy Cheddar Coins

a little bite of cheese and chile

Southerners are crazy about cheese straws or coins or sticks or fingers—any form of these melting, crumbling morsels of flour, butter, and cheese. Businesses might send their clients a sealed tin of gourmet cheese straws, and holiday visitors commonly show up with a cellophane bagful as a hostess gift. But the best ones of all are fresh out of a baker's oven, with a little extra spice from cayenne and, in this case, a hit of the addictively smoky spicy Spanish paprika known as pimentón *helping play up the potency of the sharpest cheese you can find at the grocery store. Cheese straws are supposed to be orange from using a red cheddar, but I do love the flavor of these with white Cabot Hunter's Cheddar, which is "seriously sharp."*

1 cup all-purpose flour
¼ teaspoon baking powder
1 teaspoon cayenne, or more to taste
½ teaspoon pimentón (optional)
½ cup (1 stick) butter, cold, cut in pieces
1 egg
2 cups grated extra-sharp cheddar (about 8 ounces)

1. In the bowl of a food processor, combine the flour, baking powder, cayenne, and pimentón. Pulse a few times to combine.

2. Add the butter and pulse until the mixture resembles coarse crumbs. Mix in the egg and cheese, and process until you have a stiff dough.

3. Divide the dough into 4 pieces and roll them into logs about 1 inch thick. Wrap them in wax paper and chill them for 2 hours.

4. When you're ready to bake, preheat the oven to 350°F. Slice each log into coins ⅛ inch thick and arrange them on baking sheets 1 inch apart. Bake them for 8 to 10 minutes, until they are golden and crisp. Cool the coins on racks and store them in airtight containers for up to 2 weeks. Frozen, they'll stay good for up to 3 months.

Conversion Guide

Weight Equivalents

The metric weights given in this chart are not exact equivalents, but have been rounded up or down slightly to make measuring easier.

AVOIRDUPOIS	METRIC
¼ ounce	7 grams
½ ounce	15 grams
1 ounce	30 grams
2 ounces	60 grams
3 ounces	90 grams
4 ounces	115 grams
5 ounces	150 grams
6 ounces	175 grams
7 ounces	200 grams
8 ounces (½ pound)	225 grams
9 ounces	250 grams
10 ounces	300 grams
11 ounces	325 grams
12 ounces	350 grams
13 ounces	375 grams
14 ounces	400 grams
15 ounces	425 grams
16 ounces (1 pound)	450 grams
1½ pounds	750 grams
2 pounds	900 grams
2¼ pounds	1 kilogram
3 pounds	1.4 kilograms
4 pounds	1.8 kilograms

Volume Equivalents

These are not exact equivalents for American cups and spoons, but have been rounded up or down slightly to make measuring easier.

AMERICAN	METRIC	IMPERIAL
¼ teaspoon	1.2 milliliters	
½ teaspoon	2.5 milliliters	
1 teaspoon	5.0 milliliters	
½ tablespoon (1½ teaspoons)	7.5 milliliters	
1 tablespoon (3 teaspoons)	15 milliliters	
¼ cup (4 tablespoons)	60 milliliters	2 fluid ounces
⅓ cup (5 tablespoons)	75 milliliters	2½ fluid ounces
½ cup (8 tablespoons)	125 milliliters	4 fluid ounces
⅔ cup (10 tablespoons)	150 milliliters	5 fluid ounces
¾ cup (12 tablespoons)	175 milliliters	6 fluid ounces
1 cup (16 tablespoons)	250 milliliters	8 fluid ounces
1¼ cups	300 milliliters	10 fluid ounces (½ pint)
1½ cups	350 milliliters	12 fluid ounces
2 cups (1 pint)	500 milliliters	16 fluid ounces
2½ cups	625 milliliters	20 fluid ounces (1 pint)
1 quart	1 liter	32 fluid ounces

Oven Temperature Equivalents

OVEN MARK	°F	°C	GAS
very cool	250–275	130–140	½–1
cool	300	150	2
warm	325	170	3
moderate	350	180	4
moderately hot	375–400	190–200	5–6
hot	425–450	220–230	7–8
very hot	475	250	9

Recipe Index

Acknowledgments

Warmest thanks to my editor Ellie Hutton, who came in at the eleventh hour to pick up the flag and continue the good fight against all authorial sloppiness. It's been a pleasure watching you work.

Most sincere thanks to the fabulous team at STC, especially my editor Natalie Kaire, who acquired the book in the first place; Dervla Kelly, who got me swiftly and neatly into production; and art director Michelle Ishay-Cohen and publisher Leslie Stoker and everyone in the excellent, detail-oriented production and art departments.

As ever, thanks to Angela Miller and Jennifer Griffin, my business partners and friends, who keep me motivated every day.

Big kisses and hugs for the awesome Rebecca ffrench, paragon of stylists, and the terrific Sarah Copeland, who magically makes food look homemade but way, way better. Rebecca graciously opened her home to us for the photo shoot, and her lovely, sweet and funny daughters Anna and Camilla helped in every way, and even consented to appear in some photos, as did our other adorable models, Amanuel Shim, Jazarah Shim, and Chloe Trachtenberg.

Grateful love to my mother, Carolyn Parrish, who kept my own kids so I could go away and work!

Most of all, thanks and love to my dear, funny, and talented husband, who photographed this book with style, flair, and perhaps the greatest attribute: endless patience. It gets the job done in books and life.